W9-CBE-216

Ministering *to the* Mourning

WARREN *and* DAVID
WIERSBE

Ministering *to the* Mourning

A PRACTICAL GUIDE FOR PASTORS, CHURCH LEADERS, AND OTHER CAREGIVERS

MOODY PUBLISHERS
CHICAGO

All Scripture quotations, unless otherwise indicated, are taken from the *Holy Bible, New International Version®*. NIV®. Copyright© 1973, 1978, 1984 by International Bible Society. Used by permission of Zondervan Publishing House. All rights reserved.

Scripture quotations marked NASB are taken from the *New American Standard Bible®*, © Copyright The Lockman Foundation 1960, 1962, 1963, 1968, 1971, 1972, 1973, 1975, 1977, 1995. Used by permission.

Cover design: Smartt Guys
Image credit: Jim Whitmer
Editor: Betsey Newenhuyse

Library of Congress Cataloging-in-Publication Data

Wiersbe, Warren W.
    Ministering to the mourning : a practical guide for pastors, church leaders, and other caregivers / by Warren W. Wiersbe and David W. Wiersbe.—2nd ed., rev. and updated.
       p. cm.
    Includes bibliographical references and index.
    ISBN-13: 978-0-8024-1241-6 (alk. paper)
    ISBN-10: 0-8024-1241-6
    1. Church work with the bereaved. 2. Bereavement—Religious aspects Christianity. I. Wiersbe, David. II. Title.
BV4330.W545 2006
259'.6—dc22

                                                                            2005037487

We hope you enjoy this book from Moody Publishers. Our goal is to provide high-quality, thought-provoking books and publications that connect truth to your real needs and challenges. For more information on other books and products written and produced from a biblical perspective, go to www.moodypublishers.com or write to:

Moody Publishers
820 N. LaSalle Blvd.
Chicago, IL 60610

1 3 5 7 9 10 8 6 4 2

Printed in the United States of America

Dedication

To that vast
and growing family of
people who have learned
that Jesus Christ can
heal the brokenhearted,
and who want to share
this comfort with others
who desperately need it.

Contents

Preface to the
Revised Edition

The first edition of this book, *Comforting the Bereaved*, was published in 1985 as a concise manual to assist busy pastors and other providers of Christian care as they ministered to people who were sorrowing over the death of a loved one. That the book has remained in print this long shows it was meeting a need, and the generous personal responses of many of the people who used the book have further encouraged us.

Now the time has come for a completely new book that can help provide pastors with the perspectives and principles they need in order to do their jobs more effectively. So many changes have occurred in society and the church, and so much new material has enriched the field of thanatology—that is, the study of death and dying—that it's very difficult to keep current. We have retained and revised some material from the original edition, but for the most part, this is an entirely new book.

Our friend Joe Bayly is now home with the Lord, and we miss him. We have retained the foreword that he graciously wrote for the first edition.

Busy church leaders will be tempted to turn immediately to the "practical" sections of the book, but we do urge you to read the other chapters as well. It helps the caregiver to have some perspective on how death is viewed in our contemporary world.

The two of us together bring to the writing of this book some eighty years of ministry experience, yet we're conscious of how much more could be written. The bibliography will point you to additional resources for your own research. We've learned that the better equipped pastors are to comfort the bereaved, the better able they are to effectively preach and serve the entire church family. It was Alexander Maclaren, the noted British preacher, who said, "If I had to do it over, I would minister more to broken hearts."

That is a good example for all of us to follow.

—*Warren W. Wiersbe*
—*David W. Wiersbe*

Foreword

At the beginning of Jesus' ministry on earth He quoted—and said that He fulfilled—the prophecy of Isaiah 61:1: "The Spirit of the Lord is upon me, because he hath anointed me . . . to heal the brokenhearted" (Luke 4:18 KJV).

Hearts were broken then as hearts are broken now. And a prime sign that the Holy Spirit has anointed His servants (Jesus' undershepherds) today continues to be that we bring healing to the brokenhearted.

But it is not an easy part of ministry, especially for the young pastor who has experienced little personal loss. Most of us, professionals and laypersons alike, feel inadequate when confronted by a lifeless body and stunned family. What can we say to parents whose teenage son has taken his own life? whose daughter has died in a car accident? or whose child has been murdered? to the widow suddenly alone after forty years with her beloved companion?

And even before those questions can be answered, what do we know about grief? If we want to bear people's sorrows, we cannot be ignorant of the forms grief takes.

This book provides biblical, practical answers to those and many other questions that fill the mind confronted by overwhelming loss and grief.

For the pastor, suggestions about visitation, the funeral service (including texts and outlines), and long-term ministry to survivors greatly increase the book's value.

One of the most encouraging verses at a time of loss is Isaiah 63:9: "In all their affliction He was afflicted, and the angel of His presence saved them" (NASB).

Through understanding and applying this book, God's servant may become His angel (messenger) to those who are brokenhearted, saving them from despair.

Thank God a day is coming when tears shall cease and death shall be destroyed.

—Joseph Bayly

Death and Contemporary American Culture

It's becoming more and more difficult to minister to grieving people, because in their attempts to enjoy life, many of them are denying death. Mention death and the average person responds something like comedian Woody Allen: "It's not that I'm afraid to die. I just don't want to be there when it happens." There are no funeral homes in shopping malls to remind us of our mortality; and if there were, the salespeople would have to hand out free coffee to keep shoppers from looking the other way. With one hand gripping the steering wheel and the other holding a cell phone, most people breeze their way through the day and never consider that it might be their last.

Ours is a culture that insists that we remain young, no matter how old we are. As for death, don't mention it! We live in a society that invents harmless antiseptic words for death—"going into the light," "passing away," "released," and so on. But avoiding the word doesn't eliminate the experience.

The Bible looks death squarely in the face: "Yet as surely as the LORD lives and as you live, there is only a step between me and death"

(1 Samuel 20:3). A step—not a mile, not light-years, just a step. The Episcopal *Book of Common Prayer* burial service puts it this way: "In life we are in death." But how many people actually believe this?

This attitude of denial is strange because world events shout "death" at us day after day. How can we deny death when 2,500,000 people die in the United States each year, and their names are listed in hometown obituary columns? About 13,000 of these people are shot—murdered—and another 17,000 deliberately shoot themselves. Sixty million people died in World War II. Over six million Jews died in the Holocaust. Watch the news on television and you may actually see people being burned to death, shot to death, or blown to bits. Let death claim a prominent person—President Reagan, the Pope, Elvis Presley, or Princess Diana—and the world follows the television reports for days, maybe weeks. As of this writing, lives are being lost in conflicts around the world daily. *Violence and death are an accepted part of contemporary life, yet people still believe it won't happen to them.*

Why this self-imposed blindness?

PEOPLE GROW HARDENED TO THE FACT OF DEATH

No matter how you get your information—television, radio, newspapers, e-mail, or Internet sources—you can't escape the rapidity and immediacy of today's news reports. We learn about suicide bombings in Baghdad or Jerusalem, or about an angry ex-employee who shot his boss and two innocent bystanders. Perhaps a violent mob scene after a soccer game left twenty people dead and many more injured. A gang fight erupted in the inner city and claimed thirteen lives, including the lives of two policemen. A couple of teenagers shot a dozen students and three teachers on a high school campus and then took their own lives.

You can't be constantly exposed to this kind of information without something happening to your inner person. Eventually the news may totally overwhelm you, and you will throw up your hands in desperation and stop listening and looking. Or the news may gradually harden you and slowly rob you of the sensitivity of heart that we all need if we're going to be emotionally balanced and build healthy personal relationships. Like guards in a death camp, people can see and hear so much that is horrible and inhuman that they get used to it, to the point where they're able to tell jokes as they stack up the corpses. In his poem "Man Was Made to Mourn," Robert

Burns wrote, "Man's inhumanity to man / Makes countless thousands mourn"; but it also makes countless millions *lose* the ability to mourn.

In her article "TV's Love Affair with Death" in the March 25, 2001, issue of the *New York Times*, Wendy Lessner makes some telling points. "Television blurs our sense of what death means, making it hard to distinguish visibility from survival, biological dissolution from corporate termination, rerun from afterlife. . . . Nestled in your living room, that little box is designed to minimize any sense of public responsibility, any sense of shame. All your reactions to it can be safely private; you can be as grossed out or as coldhearted or as maudlin as you like, and no one else needs to know."

PEOPLE BELIEVE THAT "DEATH IS NATURAL"

"Death is not an enemy to be conquered or a prison to be escaped," write Joseph and Laurie Braga in their foreword to *Death, the Final Stage of Growth* by Elisabeth Kubler-Ross. They call death "an integral part of our lives that gives meaning to human existence," an "invisible but friendly companion."

In *Thoughts on War and Death,* published in 1915, Sigmund Freud, the founder of psychoanalysis, wrote that "death [is] natural, undeniable, and unavoidable. In reality, however, we [are] accustomed to believe as if it were otherwise." Since humans are a part of nature, our death is obviously natural, and in that sense we are "like the beasts that perish" (Psalm 49:12, 20).

But while death is a biological fact, people are much more than bodies, and life is much more than physical functioning. Unlike the beasts that perish, humans are created in the image of God, and therefore death involves important matters such as God, judgment, and eternity. Death came into the world because of sin; and sin separated us from God. The sovereign Lord is the only One who can rescue us from the consequences that lie beyond death.

The "death is natural" school has lulled many people into a false sense of security. But 1 Corinthians 15 states that death is "the last enemy" (v. 26) and that victory over death is found only in Jesus Christ (vv. 21–58).

Elisabeth Kubler-Ross (1926–2004) was a pioneer in the field of thanatology, that branch of medicine that focuses on the terminally ill and their families. Dr. Kubler-Ross gave to the world the well-known five responses (or stages) that terminal patients usually experience as they await death: (1) shock and denial, (2) anger, (3) bargaining for more time, (4) depression, and (5) acceptance. But Kubler-Ross saw no reason why people should fear death. She compared death to the butterfly shedding its cocoon. To her, death was only a higher state of consciousness where people continued to laugh, perceive, and grow, something like being "born" into a new world or being graduated from school to a higher level. What basis she had for these convictions, she never revealed, but many people have believed her romanticized views of death and therefore are sure they need no spiritual preparation to die. While many of her insights into the "death process" are helpful to the alert caregiver, her views of what goes on after death are not always biblical.

The New Age movement has capitalized on these views as well as on the data from people who have had "out-of-body" (ecsomatic) experiences, such as those recorded and discussed in Raymond Moody's two books *Life After Life* and *Reflections on Life After Life* (1975).[1] New Age counselors also lean heavily on mystical statements from Eastern religions, what Lucy Bregman calls "glow words," words that are "filled with positive feelings, but lacking exact definition."[2] These "warm, fuzzy words" sound so soothing, but they lack authority. Carol W. Parrish-Harra opens her *New Age Handbook on Death and Dying* with an anonymous poem that illustrates our point. The person who has died tells us not to weep, because he or she is the wind blowing, the glitter on the snow, the sunlight on the grain, the refreshing rain, the circling birds, the stars. "Do not stand at my grave and cry / I am not there. I did not die."

The "out-of-body" testimonies usually emphasize the experience of seeing a bright light at the end of a tunnel and moving toward it with confidence. This explains the large number of New Age books with "light" in their titles, perhaps the most popular being *Embraced by the Light,* by Betty Eadie and Curtis Taylor (Bantam, 1994). But there are also *To Touch the Light* by Kevin Randle (New York: Windsor, 1994), *Closer to the Light* by Melvin Morse and Paul Perry (New York: Villard, 1994), and *One with the Light* by Brad Steiger (New York: Signet, 1994). That Satan can appear as an angel of light (2 Corinthians 11:13–15) never seems to enter into the discussion.

Multitudes of people no longer think Christianly about death. For many, fear of death is no longer part of their emotional equipment, although you won't see them taking risks that might end their lives. If they attend a Christian funeral and hear a biblical message, they will smile, filter out the theology, and hold tenaciously to their "glow words."

PEOPLE BELIEVE THEY ARE IN CHARGE OF LIFE AND DEATH

In 1988 the state of Oregon passed a Death with Dignity Act that allowed certain patients to request death at the hands of a physician. The assisting physician would be immune from prosecution, but the procedure must be carefully monitored and regulated by the proper authorities. All of this added up to "death with dignity," a practice that has been carried on in the Netherlands for several years, although without the same degree of medical accountability as is required in Oregon. "Euthanasia" is the official word for this procedure. *Euthanasia* comes from the Greek and means "easy death" or "good death." PAS is the code word: "physician-assisted suicide." Of course, euthanasia refers only to the *act* of dying, not to what happens to the individual after death. Physicians and legislators have no authority over people in the afterlife.

The great contemporary proponent of "mercy killing" is Dr. Jack Kevorkian, at this writing serving time in a Michigan correctional facility. He claims he assisted in at least 130 "mercy" deaths. Hollywood plans to make a film about him.

But euthanasia isn't the only current practice that gives society the idea that we're in charge of death; there is also abortion. It's estimated that in the United States alone, a million and a half unborn babies are legally killed each year. We have made the life-giving womb into a death-receiving tomb. Our society permits persons to be killed before they are born and when they get old and have no "quality life," a phrase that's difficult to define. If this kind of activity is legal, what does this say about our views of life?

The strange thing is that many people who approve of the killing of innocent unborn children and unhappy older folks are against killing convicted criminals. In some states, a criminal must kill at least two victims before being eligible for death row. This means that the life of one guilty murderer is worth the lives of two innocent citizens, which is strange mathematics indeed. The execution of a guilty criminal may not deter others from committing a capital crime, but it is a signal that the ultimate punishment is death, *because death ends all as far as this world is concerned.*

The fate of baseball legend Ted Williams has turned the media spotlight on the practice of cryonics—that is, keeping a dead body frozen for possible revival. Cryonics is another means through which humans try to have the last word over death. After Williams died on July 5, 2002, his body was shipped to an Arizona cryonics center where it was prepared and frozen, awaiting the day when science will discover how to restore dead cells and bring people back to life again. At this time, however, the cost of preparing and preserving the body is about $120,000—prohibitive to most families.

Embryonic stem cell research is yet another area in which the denial of death is practiced. This process of experimenting on embryos is called "therapeutic research," but the fact is that the embryos are destroyed in the pursuit of scientific knowledge. The word "therapeutic" applies, not to the embryo, but to the person who might benefit from what is learned. To those who believe in the sanctity of human life, embryonic stem research involves killing a person. A utilitarian perspective says that it is acceptable to take a life in order to save a life, but the word "death" rarely enters the discussion.

PEOPLE BELIEVE THE WRONG PHILOSOPHY OF LIFE

Most people aren't professional philosophers and wouldn't know a logical positivist from a moral realist, but what professional philosophers believe, teach, and write filters down to us and quietly influences our thinking and living. All writers and artists have a philosophy of life, and it's bound to show up in what they produce, be it comedy, drama, sculpture, paintings, or television specials. What we see and hear in movies and on television, as well as what we read, can subtly introduce us to some of these philosophies. If you watch enough reruns of your favorite TV series, you will discover the writers' views about a number of things, because gifted writers share their philosophy of life. Or, you can read *Sophie's Choice* by William Styron and get a short course in philosophy while following the story.

We don't talk much about existentialism nowadays, but its influence lingers. After World War II, existentialism invaded American academia and from the campus moved to the marketplace, the theater, and even the church. There is a Christian existentialism (Kierkegaard, for instance) as well as an agnostic (or atheistic) existentialism, but both schools believe that everyday existence is artificial and superficial and therefore puts people into bondage. But when individuals come to grips with the realities of life, especially death, this creates anxiety, which when accepted leads the way to freedom. This demands a courageous "leap of faith," but for most existentialists it's faith in yourself, not faith in God.

MULTITUDES OF PEOPLE NO LONGER THINK CHRISTIANLY ABOUT DEATH.

The fact of death occupies a central place in existentialism, although the agnostic existentialist has no belief in an afterlife. Karl Jaspers wrote, "To learn to live and to learn how to die are one and the same thing."[3] To them, the essence of true human existence is found in freedom, and freedom comes from self-determination, the individual's acceptance of reality and responsibility, no matter where the decisions may lead. "Man makes himself," said Jean-Paul Sartre, the existentialist philosopher, playwright, and novelist. "He isn't ready-made at the start." Existentialists like to think of themselves as self-made people.

Existentialism's emphasis on death and the anguish of life helped to produce the theater of the absurd, certain schools of modern art and experimental music, and a host of novels and plays. All of these declare the importance of the individual and his or her decisions, and the need for courage to be yourself in spite of circumstances. It's William Ernest Henley's poem "Invictus" all over again: "I am the master of my fate / I am the captain of my soul."

Students discuss Sartre's novels from high school to graduate school, and his plays are produced by drama classes, so his philosophy gets a hearing and influences people's thinking whether they know it or not.

Fascinated by such a daring approach to life, students try to display their erudition by quoting Sartre, not realizing what he's really saying. "I am condemned to be free." "Hell is other people." "Human life begins at the far side of despair." It sounds clever, but is it true?

Existentialism isn't a popular philosophy today, but the seeds sown by the songs, novels, and plays produced by existentialist writers are still bearing fruit.

> AS WE MINISTER TO PEOPLE,
> THEIR WORLDVIEW WILL EITHER
> FILTER OUT GOD OR OPEN
> THE DOOR TO HIS TRUTH.

THE WORLDLY MIND AND THE WORD OF GOD

Put all of the above together and add the allure of money, the quest for worldly success, the appetite for pleasure, and the strategy of the Evil One, and you have "the world," which is the strongest influence that affects people's minds today. The apostle John called it "the cravings of sinful man, the lust of his eyes and the boasting of what he has and does" (1 John 2:16). Many people are like the farmer in our Lord's parable who was sure he was ready to retire, only to discover that he would be summoned by God that very night (Luke 12:13–21). Most people don't know that parable, but they do practice the farmer's philosophy of life—"eat, drink, and be merry."

Our point is simply this: as we minister to people, their worldview will either filter out God or open the door to His truth. The people may not even know what's going on in their own minds, but we must be aware of the process and do our best to communicate God's truth in such a way that they will understand it and accept it. We need an understanding of the Word of God, the fullness of the Spirit of God, and a love for these people for whom Christ died.

NOTES

1. Raymond Moody, *Life After Life* (New York: Bantam Books), 1976.

2. Lucy Bregman, *Beyond Silence and Denial* (Louisville: Westminster John Knox Press, 1999), 7.

3. Quoted in *Death and Western Thought* by Jacques Choron (New York: Collier Books, 1963), 228. This book is an excellent survey of what Western philosophy teaches about death.

Death in the
Old Testament

What the culture says about death is one thing, and we need to be aware of how our people are influenced. But where we must begin, of course, in our thinking and in our ministering is with Scripture.

We who are in Christ know that if He returns before our time comes to die, we shall be privileged to follow Him home (John 11:25). God's people are always encouraged by that blessed hope (1 Thessalonians 4:13–18). Yet we must still live each day soberly, realizing that we are mortal and that death may come to us at any time. We pray, "Teach us to number our days aright, that we may gain a heart of wisdom" (Psalm 90:12).

To begin, the biblical definition of death is "the body without the spirit is dead . . ." (James 2:26). We each have a body made of dust and inhabited by a spirit given to us by almighty God (Genesis 2:7). At death, the spirit leaves the body (Genesis 35:18 NASB; Psalm 146:4), and with the life gone, the body begins to decay and return to dust (Genesis 3:19). The spirit of the believer goes to be with Christ in heaven (Philippians 1:23), while the spirit of the unbeliever goes into the "world of the dead" called sheol in the Old Testament and hades in the New Testament. More about that later.

DEATH: HISTORY AND THEOLOGY

The key passages are Genesis 3, which gives the history, and Romans 5:12–21, which explains the theology. Our first parents were warned that they would die if they ate of the Tree of the Knowledge of Good and Evil (Genesis 2:15–17; 3:2–3). They were the king and queen of the old creation, made in the image of God and given authority (dominion) to rule with God and for God (Genesis 1:26–31; Psalm 8). Eve was deceived, believed Satan's lies, and partook of the forbidden fruit and shared it with her husband. Adam was the head of the old creation, and when he sinned, all his descendants sinned in him. It is in Adam that all die (1 Corinthians 15:22), for Adam sinned deliberately, with his eyes wide open (1 Timothy 2:14).

Adam and Eve had been exercising dominion over God's creation, but now that had to change. Paul explains in Romans 5 that two other "kings" appeared on the scene: sin began to reign and death began to reign (Romans 5:14–17, 21). Adam and Eve experienced spiritual death and were separated from God, and their bodies began to die. "Therefore, just as sin entered the world through one man, and death through sin, and in this way death came to all men, because all sinned [in Adam]" (Romans 5:12).

But then a new king appeared—God's grace (Romans 5:21). God came to the garden and sought Adam and Eve. He dealt with their sin and then in His grace forgave them. He should have passed judgment and killed them, but instead, innocent animals died in their place that they might be clothed and be accepted before God. That sacrifice pointed to the Lord Jesus Christ, who died for us on the cross so that "grace might reign through righteousness to bring eternal life through Jesus Christ our Lord" (Romans 5:21). In fact, those who belong to Christ can today "reign in life" through Christ (Romans 5:17) and will one day regain their lost dominion. Death still reigns, but there's no reason why sin should reign in the life of the believer (Romans 8:1–17). God invites us to "reign in life" as we yield to the Lord (Romans 5:17).

But the law of sin and death began to produce consequences very early in human history, as recorded in Genesis. Cain killed Abel and then lied about it (Genesis 4), and Genesis 5 declares that all of Adam's descendants died, except Enoch, and the phrase "and then he died" is found eight times in this chapter. By the time you get to Genesis 6, sin has so polluted the human race that God has determined to wipe it out. But Noah found grace in the eyes of God (Genesis 6:8), and he and his family were saved by faith in God's promise. Now God's grace is going to reign! But death is still God's universal judgment of sin. No one can escape death, and Jesus Christ holds the keys of death and Hades (Revelation 1:18; see Deuteronomy 32:39). The only way to escape the eternal penalties of sin and death is to trust Him, for He is the Son of God and the Lamb of God (John 1:29, 49).

It's important to understand Satan's relationship to death. Jesus called him a murderer (John 8:44), and Hebrews 2:14 affirms that he has the power of death; but Satan can do only that which God permits (Job 1:1–2:10). Since sin eventually leads to death (James 1:15; Romans 6:23), and Satan knows how to tempt people to sin, in this sense he has the power of death. Judas, an unbeliever (John 6:70), yielded to the Devil and went out and killed himself (John 13:2, 21–30; Matthew 27:1–5). Satan tempted Ananias and Sapphira to lie about their offering, and this led to their death (Acts 5:1–11). In the church at Corinth, some of the believers who deliberately sinned became ill, and some died (1 Corinthians 11:30–31). From the Old Testament, Job's children come to mind (Job 1:8–9).

IN GOD'S HANDS

Psalm 139:13–16 teaches that both our birth and our death are in the hands of God, and Psalm 116:15 states that the death of the believer is "precious" in the sight of God. That doesn't mean that the Lord enjoys seeing His children die and their loved ones grieve, but that the death of a believer in God's sight is so personal and precious that it doesn't happen by accident. The author of Psalm 116 was in a dangerous situation. His life was threatened, but God answered his prayers and spared him. Why? Because God watches over His own for whom His Son died, and He doesn't leave their homecoming to what the world calls "chance" or "fate." Our days are already written in His book (Psalm 139:16). We can be foolish and shorten our lives, but we cannot go beyond the limits God has set.

We will leave this world empty-handed (1 Timothy 6:7; Job 1:21–22), but we can use our time, abilities, opportunities, and possessions to win others to Christ (Luke 16:9–15) and to lay up treasures in heaven (Matthew 6:19–24). Faithfulness here will honor Christ and gain His approval and reward when we see Him in heaven.

The fact of death introduces uncertainty into life, and this forces us to say, "If it is the Lord's will, we will live and do this or that" (James 4:15). It also reminds us that opportunities don't last forever and that living each day for Jesus is essential. Our friends and loved ones won't be with us forever, nor we with them, so we all ought to cherish one another and forgive one another. How many times we've heard people say after funerals, "We just didn't keep in touch—and now it's too late."

Some Bible students believe that Moses wrote Psalm 90 after Israel's great sin at Kadesh Barnea, when they failed to enter the Promised Land (Numbers 14). Note especially the descriptions of God's anger, Israel's sins, and the certainty of death. The psalm forcefully reminds us of the sovereignty of God, the frailty of mankind, the brevity of life, and the certainty of death. We desperately need God's wisdom if we hope to make a success out of this brief time we have on earth (Psalm 90:12).

Isaiah 38 records the experience of King Hezekiah when Isaiah the prophet told him he would die. The king was stunned and pled with the Lord to allow him to live, and God in His grace gave him fifteen more years. When you read the psalm Hezekiah wrote, you discover that his confrontation with death gave him a new appreciation for life (vv. 15–16), a new confidence in prayer (vv. 2–3), and a new understanding of God's love (v. 17). He saw his life as God's weaving and death as God's cutting him from the loom (v. 12). God has a perfect pattern for each life. Today we see life only from the underside and the pattern isn't clear—but one day we shall see it from God's viewpoint.

In the Old Testament, God's revelation about death and the afterlife was not given in its fullness. The Old Testament writers took death seriously, and so must we, but they were living in the shadows. It was not until the coming of Jesus Christ to earth that He "abolished death and brought life and immortality to light through the gospel" (2 Timothy 1:10 NASB). This means we must be cautious when we preach funeral messages from Job, Ecclesiastes, and some of the doleful "graveyard" psalms. These inspired texts must be understood in the full light of Christ's revelation of life and immortality.

THE MANY IMAGES OF DEATH

The Bible uses the words *die, dead,* and *death* more than 1,300 times, and it records the deaths of many people, both good and evil. Scripture also includes dozens of images and metaphors for death:

blot the name out—Exodus 32:32–33; Psalm 69:28; and see Revelation 3:5

bowl broken— Ecclesiastes 12:6

breathe your last—Gen. 25:8, 17; 35:18, 29; 49:33; Job 14:10; Psalms 39:5, 11; 62:9; 144:4 (see also Mark 15:37 and Luke 23:46)

coals going out—2 Samuel 14:7 (the end of the family)

cords entangling a person—2 Samuel 22:6; Psalms 18:4–5; 116:3

crushing a moth—Job 4:19

darkness; light put out—1 Samuel 2:9; Job 3:4–6, 9; 10:21; 12:22; 17:13; 18:5–6, 18; 21:17; 24:17; Psalm 88:12; Proverbs 13:9; 20:20; 24:20; Ecclesiastes 6:4. Note the New Testament image in 2 Timothy 1:10.

depths; drowning; swallowed up—2 Samuel 22:5; Psalms 18:4–6; 42:7; 69:2, 15; Isaiah 5:14 (1 Cor. 15:54–57); Jonah 2:5; Habakkuk 2:5

devoured—Deuteronomy 32:42; 2 Samuel 1:22; 2:26; 11:25; Isaiah 1:20; 31:8; Jeremiah 2:30; 5:17; 8:16; 12:12; 46:10, 14; Nahum 2:13. Death and the grave were sometimes personified and described as having insatiable appetites (Isaiah 5:14; Habakkuk 2:5; Proverbs 27:20; 30:15–16). God's promise was that He would swallow up death and it would be no more (see Isaiah 25:7–8; 1 Corinthians 15:54–58; Revelation 20:14; 21:4).

dust (corruption, decay)—Genesis 3:19; Job 7:21; 10:9; 17:16; 20:11; 21:26; 34:15; Psalms 7:5; 16:10 (see Acts 2:27); 22:15; 55:23; 90:3; 104:29; Proverbs 10:7; Ecclesiastes 3:20; 12:7; Isaiah 26:19; Daniel 12:2; Zephaniah 1:17

gates, doors (open, shut)—Job 3:10; 17:16; 38:17; Psalms 9:13; 107:18; Isa. 38:10 (see also Matt. 16:18)

grass, flower (frailty of humanity)—2 Kings 19:26; Job 8:12; 14:1–2; Psalms 37:1–2; 90:5–6; 92:7; 103:15–16; Isaiah 37:27; 40:6–8 (1 Peter 1:24); 51:12

the harvest—"gathered to one's people"; Genesis 25:8, 17; 35:29; 49:29, 33; Numbers 27:13; 31:2; Judges 2:10; 2 Kings 22:20; 2 Chronicles 34:28; Job 5:26; 9:22; Psalm 129:5–7; Jeremiah 9:22 (which may be the origin of the familiar phrase "the grim reaper")

"king of terrors"—Job 18:14. Read the entire chapter. It's a vivid description of death capturing a victim. See how many pictures you can find in this dramatic chapter. Scripture does not minimize the terrors of death for the unbeliever, but we must use discretion and handle such images carefully. If you are constrained to preach judgment, be sure you have a broken heart and tears. Please don't preach hell as though you're happy people are going there.

pitcher broken—Ecclesiastes 12:6

rider on a pale horse—Revelation 6:8

shadow—Job 3:4–5; 10:21–22; 28:3; 34:22; 38:17; Psalms 23:4; 44:19; Isaiah 9:2 (Matthew 4:13–16); Jer. 2:6; Amos 5:8

shroud—Isa. 25:7

sleep—The phrase "sleep with one's fathers" or "rest with one's fathers" is used many times in the Old Testament as an image of natural peaceful death, joining one's ancestors in the realm of the dead. It is the body that sleeps, not the soul. Our English word "cemetery" comes from the Greek and means "sleeping place." Genesis 15:15; 47:30; Deuteronomy 31:16; 1 Kings 1:21; 2:10; 11:43; 14:20, 31; 15:8, 24; 16:6, 28; 22:40, 50; 2 Kings 8:24; 9:28; 10:35; 13:9, 13; 14:16, 22, 29; 15:7, 22, 38; 16:20; 20:21; 21:18; 22:20; 24:6; 2 Chronicles 9:31; 12:16; 14:1; 16:13; 21:1; 26:2, 23; 27:9; 28:27; Job 3:13; Pss. 7:5; 13:3; 49:19; 76:5; 90:5; Isa. 26:19; Jeremiah 51:39, 57; Daniel 12:2, 13 *snare, trap*—2 Sam. 22:6; Psalm 18:5; Proverbs 13:14; 14:27

spinal cord cut—Ecclesiastes 12:6

stumbling and slipping—2 Samuel 22:37; Psalms 18:36; 26:12; 37:31; 56:13; 116:8

swept away—Psalms 90:5

tent taken down—Job 4:21; 18:6, 14; Isaiah 38:12 (see 2 Corinthians 5:1; 2 Peter 1:13–14)

thief—Job 18:13–14; Isaiah 38:10; Jeremiah 9:21

tree chopped down—Job 14:7–9

water spilled or poured out—2 Samuel 14:14; Job 14:10–12; 24:18–19; Psalms 22:14; 79:3; Isaiah 53:12. (See the image of the drink offering in Matthew 26:28; Mark 14:24; Luke 22:20; Philippians 2:17; 2 Timothy 4:6.)

weaving removed from the loom—Isaiah 38:12 (Psalm 139:15 uses weaving to picture pregnancy)

While we're focusing on images, be sure to note in the book of Job the pictures of the swiftness and brevity of life. They include the weaver's shuttle (7:6), a breath (7:7), a passing cloud (7:9, and see James 4:14), a swift messenger (9:25), a swift ship and flying eagle (9:26), a withering flower (14:2), a passing shadow (14:2), and a dream vanished (20:8–9).

THE JEWISH WAY OF DEATH

In Jewish society, for a dead body to lie unburied was disgraceful (1 Kings 13:22), and for a dead person not to be mourned publicly was humiliating (Jeremiah 16:1–7). Even the corpses of criminals were given decent burials (Deuteronomy 21:22–23). Because of the climate and the fact that dead bodies of both humans and animals were considered unclean (Numbers 19:11–16; Leviticus 11:1ff.), the dead were buried as soon as possible, usually on the day of death (Acts 5:1–11).

Immediately after death, the deceased person's eyes were closed by a family member and the body washed and then wrapped in cloths impregnated with spices. The body lay in state in the home so friends could pay their respects and express their sorrow along with the grieving family (Acts 9:32–42). The visitors usually brought gifts of food to the home. Before sundown, the body was placed on a simple bier and carried to the burial place (2 Samuel 3:31; 2 Chronicles 16:14; Luke 7:14). Unlike the Egyptians, the Jews did not embalm the dead, and unlike some of their pagan neighbors, they did not cremate dead bodies. The family of the deceased would fast until sunset, but their mourning would continue.

PLEASE DON'T PREACH

HELL AS THOUGH

YOU'RE HAPPY PEOPLE

ARE GOING THERE.

Personal and communal mourning was an important part of Jewish funerals, and it would continue for a week. If a parent died, the children would mourn for a month and then pay special tribute annually at the grave. Mourners expressed their grief in many ways: weeping, tearing their garments, sitting in the dust, scattering dust on their heads, fasting, wearing sackcloth, beating their breast, wailing, and going barefoot, and women might unbind their hair (2 Samuel 1:11–12; 3:31; 13:31; 15:30; Job 1:20; Isaiah 22:12; Ezekiel 7:18 and 27:31; Joel 1:8; Amos 8:10; Micah 1:16). You could also hire professional mourners to augment this display of grief (Mark 5:38). Sometimes special songs were written to express grief for the departed. David wrote one in honor of Saul and Jonathan (2 Samuel 1:17–27) and also to lament the death of Abner (2 Samuel 3:33–34), and Jeremiah wrote one after the untimely death of King Josiah (2 Chronicles 35:25).

The Jews were not allowed to adopt the excessive godless practices of the Gentile nations, such as cutting themselves (Leviticus 19:28; 21:5; Deuteronomy 14:1–3). This reminds us that Christian believers today are expected to mourn, but not "like the rest of men, who have no hope" (1 Thessalonians 4:13). Even in our grief, God should be glorified. The prayers and encouragement of other believers is an important part of the healing process, and Christians must learn to "mourn with those who mourn" (Romans 12:15).

Families usually buried their dead in caves or else had tombs carved out of the soft limestone rock. The poorer people buried in the earth and identified the graves with suitable stone markings. Sometimes pillars were erected as memorials to the dead (Genesis 35:20; 2 Samuel 18:18; 2 Kings 23:17). Abraham paid a large price for a burial place for his wife, Sarah (Genesis 23), the first funeral recorded in Scripture. (Sarah is also the only woman in Scripture whose age at death is recorded.) By the time we get to the end of Genesis, the tomb also contains the remains of Abraham (Genesis 25:1–11), Isaac, Rebekah, Leah, and Jacob (Genesis 49:29–33; 50:13). The first book in the Old Testament closes with six corpses in a tomb, but the first book in the New Testament closes with an empty tomb, for Jesus is risen from the dead! The gospel message is not only that Christ died for our sins, but also that He has risen from the dead.

> THE FIRST BOOK IN THE OLD TESTAMENT
> CLOSES WITH SIX CORPSES IN A TOMB,
> BUT THE FIRST BOOK IN THE NEW
> TESTAMENT CLOSES WITH AN EMPTY TOMB.

Jacob was honored with an extended time of mourning and an elaborate burial (Genesis 50:1–14)—this was because he was the father of Joseph, the savior of Egypt. Joseph was also embalmed and placed in a coffin, but he was not buried until after the Jews had conquered the Promised Land (Genesis 50:24–26 and 33:19; Exodus 13:19; Joshua 24:32). The Jewish people must have carefully cared for and cherished that coffin, for during their difficult years in Egypt and in the wilderness, it reminded them of God's promise to care for them and take them to their own land (Genesis 15:16; 46:1–4; 48:21–22). Though they suffered much, they were a people who had hope.

Apart from the deaths and burials mentioned above, here is a list of other persons whose departures and burials are recorded in the Old Testament.

DEBORAH (Gen. 35:8)	ASAHEL (2 Sam. 2:32)
RACHEL (Gen. 35:16–20)	ABNER (2 Sam. 3:27)
ISAAC (Gen. 35:27–29)	AHITHOPHEL (2 Sam. 17:23)
NADAB AND ABIHU	DAVID (1 Kings 2:1–11;
(Lev. 10:1–2)	1 Chron. 29:26–28)
MIRIAM AND AARON	JOAB (1 Kings 2:34)
(Num. 20:1, 22–29)	SOLOMON (1 Kings 11:41–43)
MOSES (Deut. 34)	JEROBOAM AND REHOBOAM
JOSHUA (Josh. 24:29–30)	(1 Kings 14:19–20, 31)
GIDEON (Judg. 8:32)	ASA (1 Kings 15:23–24)
SAMSON (Judg. 16:23–31)	AHAB (1 Kings 22:37–40)
ELI (1 Sam. 4:14–18)	AHAZIAH (2 Kings 9:27–28)
SAMUEL (1 Sam. 25:1)	JEHU (2 Kings 10:34–36)
SAUL AND HIS SONS	JOASH (2 Kings 12:19–21)
(1 Sam. 31:10–13; 2 Sam.	JOSIAH (2 Kings 23:29–30)
21:12–14)	

THE LAND OF THE DEAD

Each of the nations in the ancient world had its name for the "land of the dead." For the Jews, it was *sheol*, and for the Greeks, *hades*. Many scholars believe that the sheol of the Old Testament is the equivalent of the hades of the New Testament, and the compound term *sheol/hades* is often used as a name for this awesome place. The word *sheol* is found sixty-six times in the Hebrew Bible and is translated a number of ways, primarily the grave, death, the pit, and the depths. Some students feel it would be better just to transliterate the words as we have done here and let the reader work out the definition from the context.

The descriptions of the land of the dead are not encouraging. It's a place of darkness (Job 17:13; 18:18; Lamentations 3:6), dust and worms (Job 17:12–16), loneliness (Psalm 31:17–18; Isaiah 47:5), no praise of God (Psalms 6:5; 30:9), cut off from God's care (Psalm 88:1–12), and awesome silence (Psalms 94:17; 115:17). Why would God send His righteous saints to a place like that?

If sheol/hades is just the grave, then the reference is only to the body; but there are texts that in their descriptions surely go beyond simply a place of burial. Furthermore, while there are texts that tell us that the wicked go to sheol/hades (Psalms 6:5; 30:3, 7; 88:3–6; Proverbs 9:18), the righteous are there also (Genesis 37:35). Our Lord's description of hades in Luke 16:19–31 indicates that both the righteous and the wicked are in hades, but that the righteous are enjoying blessing while the wicked are suffering pain. Some students believe that at some time after His resurrection, Jesus ascended to the Father and took the righteous inhabitants of hades to heaven with Him.

However we interpret the Old Testament descriptions of *sheol/hades*, we must not include our speculations in a funeral message, for people going through the valley are looking for certainties, and we have plenty of those in Scripture. Even old covenant saints had the certainty of a future with God, so let's consider those passages.

A DIM BUT CERTAIN HOPE

When death began to "reign" after Adam's sin, the Lord performed a miracle that's recorded in the Genesis 5 obituary: one man didn't die! "Enoch walked with God; then he was no more, because God took him away" (Genesis 5:24). Hebrews 11:5 says, "By faith Enoch was taken from this life, so that he did not experience death." Centuries later the prophet Elijah was also taken to heaven without experiencing death (2 Kings 2:9–12). These two men bear witness to the reality of heaven and the assurance that those who live by faith in the Lord will one day go there.

According to Hebrews 11:10–16, Abraham and the other patriarchs had their eyes set on a heavenly city that God had promised them. One day they would exchange their temporary tents for a permanent city designed and constructed by the Lord. Certainly they passed this great truth along to their descendants. During his last message to his sons just before he died, Jacob cried out to God, "I look for your deliverance, O LORD" (Genesis 49:18). The tense of the verb indicates "I have trusted and I am still trusting." He was referring to the hope of leaving earth and going to be with the Lord in heaven. Does that sound like a man who didn't know where he was going?

Throughout the Old Testament, Jehovah God is described as "the living God" and is contrasted to the dead idols of the heathen (Deuteronomy 5:26; Joshua 3:10; 1 Samuel 17:28; 2 Kings 19:16; Psalms 18:6; 42:2; 84:2; Jeremiah 10:10; Daniel 6:26; Hosea 1:10). How could the living God permit His people to die and be forgotten as their bodies turn to dust in the ground? Jesus made this clear: "He is not the God of the dead but of the living" (Matthew 22:32).

Job 19:25–26 is a great promise of future life. In the Psalms, too, the Lord gives us glimpses of what is to come. Psalm 16:7–11 is a messianic promise, quoted by Peter in his Pentecost sermon (Acts 2:25–28), but it is true of God's people as well. Other texts include Psalms 17:15; 23:6; 49:14–15; 71:20; and 73:23–26; Isaiah 25:8 and 26:19; Daniel 12:2; and Hosea 13:14.

DEATH 'UNDER THE SUN'

When Solomon wrote Ecclesiastes, he was looking at life "under the sun," a phrase he used twenty-nine times. (He also used "under heaven" three times.) His viewpoint is strictly secular. Even with all his wisdom, he saw only what other people saw and drew conclusions that weren't always accurate. Therefore, be careful when you choose a text from Ecclesiastes. When Solomon finally got around to moving "over the sun" and getting God's perspective, his philosophy changed.

In his examination of life "under the sun," Solomon decided that there were three insoluble problems: the unfairness of life, our lack of understanding of what's going on, and the inevitability of death. The certainty of death is a repeated topic and is an important part of the puzzle Solomon was trying to solve. "What's the sense of being wise and getting wealthy and powerful," he asks, "if you're going to die and leave everything to somebody else? Your successor might be a fool and lose everything." Of course, the Christian would answer, "What you have in life and what you do with it determines what the Lord will do with you after you die. Life is a stewardship: we can waste it, spend it, or invest it in that which is eternal."

When Solomon writes that humans are like animals (Ecclesiastes

3:18–20), he isn't denying the fact that humans are made in the image of God. He's writing only about death: animals die and humans die, and the bodies of both ultimately go to the same place, the ground, and turn to dust. When you die, you can't take it with you (5:15–16), so why bother to acquire it? But material things aren't the most important things in life. It's good to have what money can buy, *provided you don't lose what money can't buy!*

Solomon understood the mystery of death. Nobody can control the wind, and nobody has the power to postpone the day of death (8:8). Nobody knows the day of his or her death, so we had all better live by faith and do what the Lord tells us to do (9:1–3). Note that Solomon had a pessimistic view of the realm of the dead (9:3–10).

Ecclesiastes 12 vividly describes the gradual decline of an aged person's physical faculties, resulting in eventual death. The arms and hands shake and the shoulders and knees weaken. The teeth decay and fall out and the vision begins to fade. Hearing fails. You can't sleep as long as you once did but "wake up with the birds." Your voice starts to quaver, your hair turns white, and you just drag along slowly as you walk. You don't have a good appetite, and one day, you go to your eternal home. The silver chain breaks that holds the golden bowl (a lamp), and the lamp falls and is broken. The wheel at the well breaks and the water pitcher shatters, and it's all over. One day the machinery of life will slow down and stop for all of us. Then what?

There are many provocative and descriptive texts in Ecclesiastes that can open the way for preaching the gospel of Jesus Christ, but keep in mind that a funeral message must not become a detailed exposition. Solomon set out to examine life and discover what was really worth living for, and this is something all people must do before they die. Paul had the right idea: "For to me, to live is Christ and to die is gain" (Philippians 1:21).

Death in the New Testament

The pagans of the New Testament world were very like many in our world today. Despite their many achievements, the brilliance of their philosophies, and the cleverness of their inventions, the pagan world was helpless in the face of death. Like people today, the ancient world clung to false religions, empty traditions, and popular lies, and chose not to think too much about death. The Greek dramatist Aeschylus wrote, "Once a man dies, there is no resurrection," and the Greek philosophers in Athens laughed at Paul when he proclaimed the resurrection of Jesus Christ (Acts 17:16–33).

The Greek poet Theocritus wrote, "There is hope for those who are alive, but those who have died are without hope." Archaeologists found this epitaph on an ancient tomb: "I was not—I became—I am not—I care not." Pessimism ruled the day. "The best thing is not to be born," said one writer. "The second best is to escape life as soon as possible." The people were "without hope and without God in the world" (Ephesians 2:12). Then Jesus Christ, the Son of God, appeared on the scene!

"SITTING IN THE DARKNESS"

Sad to say, except for a small believing remnant, many of the Jewish people in the first century had very little confidence when it came to death and the afterlife. The Pharisees believed in the resurrection, but the Sadducees denied it. When Jesus began His ministry in Galilee, "The people who were sitting in darkness saw a great Light, and those who were sitting in the land and shadow of death, upon them a Light dawned" (Matthew 4:12–16 NASB). Matthew was quoting Isaiah 9:2, but Isaiah wrote "walking" and "living" and not "sitting." From Isaiah's day (700 BC) to the time Messiah arrived, the people who had once walked and lived in darkness had completely given up and were "sitting" in the darkness, helpless and hopeless.

> ARCHAEOLOGISTS FOUND THIS EPITAPH
> ON AN ANCIENT TOMB: 'I WAS NOT—
> I BECAME—I AM NOT—I CARE NOT.'

Jesus ushered in a new era with a living hope, and it's our privilege to preach that hope today. He "destroyed [broke the power of] death and has brought life and immortality to light through the gospel" (2 Timothy 1:10). In our Lord's time, the Jewish people followed the burial customs pretty much as the Jews did in the Old Testament. No sooner had Jairus's young daughter died than the mourners arrived and began to weep and wail (Matthew 9:23–25). However, Jesus never criticized genuine mourning, and He Himself wept at the tomb of Lazarus (John 11:33–35). See also Acts 7:57–8:2. Yes, believers who die go to be with the Lord, but those who are left behind sorely miss them, and mourning is our normal response to painful separation.

IMAGES OF DEATH IN THE NEW TESTAMENT

Some of the Old Testament images of death are repeated in the New Testament but given new significance.

sleep—Paul calls the Christian dead "those who have fallen asleep in him [Jesus]" (1 Thessalonians 4:14). However, nowhere are we told that Jesus "fell asleep" in death, because He tasted the full impact of death on the cross. Because of His sufferings, death for us has lost its terror and its sting and may be compared to falling asleep. Of course, it is the body of the believer that sleeps; the spirit goes to be with Christ (Acts 7:60). See also Matthew 9:24; Mark 5:39; Luke 8:52; John 11:11; Acts 13:36; 1 Corinthians 11:30; 15:6, 18, 20, 51; 1 Thessalonians 4:13–15; 5:10. To "die in the Lord" means to be at rest (Revelation 14:13).

absent from the body—The spirit departs from the body and goes to be with Christ (2 Corinthians 5:8; James 2:26). In 2 Corinthians 5:1–4, Paul intimates that there is an "intermediate body" of some kind as saints await the resurrection, but assures us that one day we will have permanent immortal glorified bodies.

changing clothes—1 Corinthians 15:50–58. See also 2 Corinthians 5:1–4; Philippians 3:20–21; and 1 John 3:1–3.

departure—The Greek word gives us the English word "analysis," and it was used to describe a soldier taking down a tent and moving on, a ship setting sail, the unyoking of oxen, and the solving of a problem. Simeon used it of his own death (Luke 2:29), and Paul used it in Philippians 1:23 and 2 Timothy 4:6. For the believer, death means the battles are over, the burdens are set aside, and we move to a better country where we will understand the mysteries that perplexed us in life. "Taking down a tent" is found also in 2 Corinthians 5:1–4 and 2 Peter 1:13–14.

exodus—On the Mount of Transfiguration, this is what Jesus called His own death (Luke 9:31). Just as Moses had led the people of Israel out of Egyptian bondage, so our Lord leads sinners out of bondage through His death and resurrection (Colossians 1:12–14). Peter used the word to describe his impending death (2 Peter 1:15).

> **going home**—Before He began His ministry, our Lord was a carpenter (Mark 6:3), and today He is building a home for us in heaven (John 14:1–6). When we are "away from the body," we are "at home with the Lord" (2 Corinthians 5:6–9).
>
> **planting a seed**—Jesus referred to His own death and burial as the planting of a seed that would produce a glorious harvest (John 12:20–28). In 1 Corinthians 15:35–49, Paul used the same image with reference to the resurrection of the human body. Note also that Paul connects the resurrection with the Feast of Firstfruits that followed Passover (1 Corinthians 15:20, 23). We will deal further with the seed image later in this chapter.

WHAT JESUS TAUGHT ABOUT DEATH

Our Lord's teaching about death was usually in connection with a miracle He performed, a question asked, or a trap set by His enemies. We will take His teachings in the chronological order followed by most Gospel harmonies.

JOHN 5:24–29. Jesus had healed on the Sabbath, and this aroused the opposition of the Jewish leaders. His reply was simply that He was doing only that which His Father was doing (5:17). The difference was that the Father did miracles gradually, while the Son did them instantly. The Father is still turning water into wine, multiplying grain, and healing bodies, but we don't necessarily see these things occurring. If the religious rulers opposed Him for a simple miracle of healing, what would they do when He raised the dead? Jesus deals with four different resurrections: the spiritual resurrection of lost sinners who trust Him (5:24–25; Ephesians 2:1–10); His own resurrection (5:26); the future resurrection of believers to glory (5:28–29); and the future resurrection of the lost to judgment (5:29; Revelation 20:11–15). Jesus announced that He was the victor over death.

LUKE 7:11–17. Two crowds met at the city of Nain, the crowd following Jesus and the crowd following a corpse being carried to the cemetery. Everybody in the world today is in one of those two crowds. The widowed mother was burying the future of her family, because this was her only son. (Jesus was also an only Son.) Jesus stopped the procession and spoke life to the dead man, who sat up and began to talk. It didn't take long for the news of this miracle to spread. This is our Lord's first recorded resurrection miracle.

MATTHEW 12:38–40. When the religious leaders asked Jesus for a sign from heaven, they were rejecting the miracles they saw Him do on earth. They wanted miracles such as Moses did in Egypt and the wilderness. The only sign He offered Israel was His death, burial, and resurrection. This is what Jonah experienced, and it was powerful enough to impress the people of Nineveh. Earlier in His ministry, Jesus had predicted His death and resurrection (John 2:18–21), and He would mention Jonah again in Matthew 16:1–4. Note that it was the resurrection—the sign of Jonah—that the apostles preached in Acts 2–12.

MATTHEW 9:18–26; MARK 5:22–43; LUKE 8:41–56. The raising of Jairus's daughter was His second recorded resurrection miracle. The widow's son had been dead less than a day and the girl less than an hour. When Jesus came to Bethany, Lazarus had been in the tomb four days (John 11:17). Which of these corpses was the most dead? A foolish question, of course, because there are no degrees of death, only degrees of decay. All lost sinners are dead, but some are more decayed than others. Jesus referred to her condition as "sleeping" and used the same image for the death of Lazarus (John 11:11). As at Nain, Jesus raised the dead by speaking the word (John 5:24). The widow's son gave evidence of life by sitting up and speaking, the girl by walking and receiving food. The compassion and the power of Jesus are seen in these miracles, and they are also vivid pictures of the salvation of lost souls.

MATTHEW 10:1–8. Jesus gave the Twelve authority to raise the dead, a fact not recorded in Mark or Luke. The ability to perform special miracles marked them as true apostles of Jesus Christ (Hebrews 2:1–4; Romans 15:19; 2 Corinthians 12:12).

MATTHEW 14:1–13. Herod's murder of John the Baptist must have deeply affected our Lord, so He took the disciples away with Him for a quiet time of retreat. Herod wanted to see Jesus and thought He was John raised from the dead. All of this must have reminded Jesus of His own impending sufferings and death. The leaders of Israel were guilty of three murders: they allowed John the Baptist to be killed and did nothing to deliver him; they asked for Jesus to be killed; and they themselves killed Stephen (Acts 7:55–60). See how their sins became worse!

JOHN 6. The day after He fed the five thousand, Jesus preached a sermon on the Bread of Life in the Capernaum synagogue. The Jews wanted a greater sign, like Moses bringing bread down from heaven, but Jesus told them He was the "bread of life" that came down from heaven. Moses fed only the Israelites and sustained their lives, but Jesus *gives life to the whole world.* Even more, He gives His life for the whole world. The one who trusts Him will live forever!

Please don't read the Lord's Supper (Eucharist, Communion) into "eating His flesh and drinking His blood." Why would Jesus discuss the supper with a crowd of unbelieving Jews when He hadn't even mentioned it to His own followers? Furthermore, why would He teach that we must partake of His flesh and blood in order to be saved and remain saved? We partake of Christ by receiving His words, a truth that Peter understood (John 6:60–69). The main lesson is clear: to participate in His life now and the resurrection unto life in the future, we must believe in Jesus Christ and receive Him within, just as the body receives food. He is the Bread of Life.

MATTHEW 16:13–17:9; MARK 8:27–9:10; LUKE 9:18–36. After Peter's confession of faith, Jesus began to teach the disciples clearly about His coming death and resurrection. Fulfilling His promise (Matthew 16:28; Mark 9:1; Luke 9:27), a week later He took Peter, James, and John with Him to the mount, where He was joined by Moses and Elijah and was transfigured before them. Jesus had just spoken about His suffering, and now He would display His glory. ("Suffering" and "glory" are repeated themes in Peter's epistles.)

On three occasions, Jesus took Peter, James, and John alone with Himself: the home of Jairus, when He raised the girl from the dead; the

Mount of Transfiguration; and the Garden of Gethsemane, when He prayed to the Father. In chapter 18 of his excellent book *The Crises of the Christ,* G. Campbell Morgan points out that all three of these events have to do with death: Jesus was victorious over death, glorified in death, and submissive to death. These lessons would speak especially to James, the first apostolic martyr (Acts 12:1–2), and to Peter and John, who suffered for the Lord's sake.

The transfiguration teaches us that there is life after death, for there were Moses and Elijah who had died centuries before! It also reminds us that death for the believer means glory with the Lord and from the Lord (John 17:22–24). We shall see His glory and share it forever!

LUKE 12:13–34. Jesus never said it was a sin to be prosperous; some very godly people named in Scripture were rich. But He warned against the love of money and using wealth to measure values. The parable illustrates 1 Timothy 6:17–19. When we die, we take nothing with us. Note the Lord's sermon to His disciples (vv. 22–34).

LUKE 16. The parable (vv. 1–15) teaches the right use of wealth: invest it making friends for the Lord (winning the lost), so that when you die, they will welcome you into heaven. The rest of the chapter may be an account of a true event that only Jesus could know, and it teaches the wrong use of wealth. Wealth can either help bring people to heaven or send people to hell. This account supports the view that sheol/hades had two sections—paradise for the saved and punishment for the lost—and that there was no way to cross from one part to the other. The fact that Enoch and Elijah went directly to heaven, and that Moses and Elijah came down to earth from heaven, indicates that the people of God did go to heaven before our Lord's resurrection and ascension. The lost who have died are not in hell but in sheol/hades, awaiting the resurrection and final judgment (Revelation 20:11–15). Sheol/hades is the jail; hell is the penitentiary. This account also teaches that God doesn't send the dead back to warn the living. The witness of God's Word is all the evidence they need, if they will accept it. Finally, nothing anybody does on earth can change the circumstances of lost people who have died, whose spirits are in the realm of the dead.

JOHN 11. The raising of Lazarus from the dead was undoubtedly the greatest miracle Jesus performed during His three years of ministry. It was the miracle that so irritated the religious leaders that they began to plot to put Him to death (11:45–54). The Jews believed that the human spirit could return to the body of the deceased within three days of death, so Jesus waited four days after Lazarus's death to come to his aid. From the beginning of this event, Jesus assured Mary and Martha that the most important thing was the glory of God (11:4, 40). Jesus was surely glorified more by raising Lazarus from the dead than by healing his sickness. That such trials should come to a family that Jesus dearly loved (11:5, 36) assures us that we must not interpret trials as evidence that God has forsaken us (Romans 8:35–39).

Three times in Scripture Mary is found at the feet of Jesus. She sat at His feet to learn (Luke 10:38–42); she fell at His feet to weep and to share her burden (John 11:32–35); and she knelt at His feet to anoint Him for His burial (John 12:1–8). Both Martha and Mary said, "Lord, if you had been here . . ." (11:21, 32), and many a grieving saint has said, "If only!" But the Lord was in full control, and they had no cause for being upset.

Jesus raised Lazarus by the power of His word (11:43–44). That word also enabled Lazarus to move to the door of the tomb, for he was bound hand and foot. None of the spoken words of Lazarus are recorded, but he was still a witness to the power of Jesus. People who had seen Lazarus dead had only to see him alive and they believed on Jesus (11:45; 12:9–11, 17–19). This also irritated the religious leaders.

Jesus was deeply moved as He stood at the tomb of Lazarus (11:33, 38). "Jesus wept" (11:35) is a verse that is brief but profound, and it reveals the tender heart of our Great High Priest (Hebrews 2:14–18; 4:14–16). "In all their affliction He was afflicted" (Isaiah 63:9 NASB). Society may claim that "real men don't cry," but the most real Man who ever walked the earth wept with His friends at the tomb of Lazarus—*even though He knew He would raise him from the dead!*

Being an orthodox Jew, Martha believed in a future resurrection, but Jesus assured her that He was the resurrection and the life (John 11:21–27). He moved this precious and comforting truth out of the Old Testament shadows and into the bright light, out of a creed and into a loving person, and out of the future and into the present. In our times of crushing sorrow, we can experience His resurrection power today

(Philippians 3:10). Having conquered death, Jesus lives according to "the power of an indestructible life" (Hebrews 7:16); so, as long as Jesus is alive, we know our Christian dead are with Him and will one day experience resurrection glory. Those believers who are alive when He returns shall never die!

Jesus prevented a funeral in the home of Jairus, interrupted a funeral at Nain, and removed all the evidences of a funeral at Bethany. Hallelujah, what a Savior!

MATTHEW 22:23–33; MARK 12:18–27; LUKE 20:27–39. The Sadducees did not believe in angels, spirits, or the resurrection of the dead (Acts 23:6–8), and they tried to trap Jesus by describing a really foolish scenario about seven brothers who successively married the same woman and then died. Whose wife would she be in the resurrection? Jesus explained that one of the purposes of marriage in this world is the continuation of the race so that children might be born to replace the people who die. But in the next life, there will be no death, so there is no need for marriage and the bearing of children.

The phrase "like the angels" doesn't mean that believers become angels when they go to heaven, because our standing in Christ makes us higher than the angels. "We shall be like him" (1 John 3:2). The marriage relationship will not exist in heaven. Jesus then silenced the Sadducees by quoting Exodus 3:6 and proving that Jehovah is the God of the living, for if the patriarchs were nothing but dust, how could the Lord be their God? No, their spirits were with the Lord in that country they had anticipated all their lives (Hebrews 11:9–16). The Lord is the God of the individual and the God of the living.

MATTHEW 26–27; MARK 14–15; LUKE 22–23; JOHN 13–19. The death of Jesus is the focus of these passages, and the background is the death of the lamb at Passover. Jesus climaxed the Passover feast by using the bread and wine to speak of His broken body and shed blood. He is the Good Shepherd who willingly gave His life for His sheep. Most people want to forget the death of a loved one, but Jesus wants us to remember His death, for it is the very heart of the Christian faith. Jesus was able to sing a hymn before going out to the garden! In the garden, He took the cup and submitted to the will of His Father, though He was not unmindful of the suffering He was about to endure. Once we know that the end is near, is this not a good example for us to follow? How wonderful to be able to say to the Father, "I have glorified You on the earth. I have finished the work that You have given me to do" (see John 17:4).

From time to time, Jesus had taught His disciples that He would be crucified, and He explained the meaning of His death. In John's gospel we have several significant images of His death: the sacrificial lamb (1:29); the destroyed and raised temple (2:18–21); the uplifted serpent (3:14–15); the shepherd dying for the sheep (10:11–18); and the buried seed (12:20–27). He had explained that He was giving Himself as a sacrifice for the sins of the world, a ransom for many (Matthew 20:28).

In His discourse in the upper room, Jesus comforted His disciples and assured them that He would meet them again. He also assured them that He would prepare a place for them in the Father's house (John 14:1–6). Heaven is a real place, and the hope Jesus gives us is a real and lasting hope, because it is a living hope.

Judas was not a believer in Jesus Christ (John 6:66–71; 13:10–11; 17:12). In the upper room, Jesus gave him opportunity to search his heart and change his mind, but he had yielded to Satan, the deceiver and the murderer. David's treacherous counselor Ahithophel is the Old Testament version of Judas, and both men hanged themselves (2 Samuel 16:15–17:23; and see Psalms 41:9; 55:12–14, 20–21; 69:25; also John 13:18). If called to conduct a funeral for a suicide, don't use texts involving either Ahithophel or Judas or any other suicide named in Scripture. We deal with this in chapter 7.

MATTHEW 28; MARK 16; LUKE 24; JOHN 20–21. That Jesus was buried by permission of Pilate was proof that He was indeed dead. It was important to have the tomb so that on the third day it might be shown empty, except for the grave clothes He left behind, like a vacated cocoon. His resurrection is proof that the Father accepted His sacrifice for the sins of the world (Romans 4:24–25). The resurrection of Jesus Christ declares to believers that death is not the end, nor is it the victor. The people in Jerusalem knew that Jesus of Nazareth had died (Luke 24:17–24), but they didn't know that He was raised from the dead; so this became the main message of the apostles (Acts 1:21–22). The resurrection of Jesus Christ is a definite part of the gospel message (1 Corinthians 15:1–8).

When our Lord dealt with the apostle Peter after the resurrection (John 21:13–23), He said that Peter would be crucified (21:18–19), and that his death would glorify God. Peter wrote about this in his second epistle (1:12–15). He saw his death as taking down a tent and making an "exodus," using the word from Luke's transfiguration account that described the victory of Jesus in Jerusalem (see Luke 9:31). Peter referred to this event in 2 Peter 1:16–18.

Every believer should strive to glorify God both in death as well as in life (Philippians 1:20–21). Note that the word "living" is a key word in Peter's first letter: a living hope (1:3), the living Word (1:23), Christ the living stone (2:4), and believers as living stones in the temple (2:5). Finally, note the emphasis on *life* in John's gospel; the word is used thirty-six times. Christian believers can discuss death and yet focus on life, because Jesus is the resurrection and the life and holds the keys of death and hades (Revelation 1:17–18).

The Christian faith is somewhat of a paradox. Jesus died that we might have life, and as we live for Him, we die to self and sin. We share in His death and His life (Galatians 2:20; 2 Corinthians 4:7–12). This is the message that was emphasized by Paul.

THE EARLY CHURCH: POWER AND GLORY

"Jesus Christ of Nazareth, whom you crucified, is alive and is Lord and Christ!" This was the message of the apostolic church (Acts 1:21–22; 2:24–28, 32; 3:15; 5:30–32). Peter declared this truth at Pentecost and proceeded to defend it on the basis of the presence of the Holy Spirit (Joel 2:28–32) and the prophecies of David (Psalms 16:8–11; 110:1). The early church not only declared and defended the resurrection of Christ by their witness and by the Word, but they also demonstrated it by their works. The early believers healed the sick and even raised the dead, all in the name of Jesus (Acts 4:1–21). The power of the Holy Spirit is the power of the risen and exalted Christ, and apart from that power the church has no witness (Acts 1:8). How could a dead Savior send the Holy Spirit or give anybody life? Paul said that Jesus was "the first to rise from the dead" (Acts 26:23), meaning "the first to rise from the dead and never die again." He is "the firstborn from among the dead" (Colossians 1:18) and the "firstfruits of those who have fallen asleep" (1 Corinthians

15:20). At His coming, there will be a "harvest," and the dead in Christ will become like their Lord and share His glory, for the "firstfruits" is identical to the harvest that follows. See Leviticus 23:9–14.

ACTS 5:1–11. The first recorded deaths in the early church were of a husband and wife, Ananias and Sapphira, who had lied to Peter and to the Holy Spirit. The Lord took their lives, and "great fear seized the whole church and all who heard about these events" (5:11). It appears that there were no "funeral services" but that the young men wrapped up the bodies and buried them.

Why would God do such a thing? Because it was the beginning of a new stage in His work on earth, the age of the church; and at new beginnings, the Lord sometimes demonstrated His holiness and power by publicly judging sinners. After giving the law at Sinai, God severely judged those who had disobeyed it (Exodus 34:15–35). No sooner had the tabernacle been dedicated than God killed Nadab and Abihu for offering unauthorized incense (Leviticus 10:1–5). Once the Jews were in the Promised Land, God killed Achan for stealing spoil from Jericho (Joshua 7). When David brought the ark of the covenant to Jerusalem at the beginning of his reign, Uzzah was slain for touching the ark (2 Samuel 6:1–15). Now at the beginning of the church age, God warned His people not to lie to Him.

ACTS 6–7. The name "Stephen" means "a victor's crown," and he won his crown by laying down his life for Jesus (Revelation 2:10). He was the church's first martyr. He began by serving food to the widows in the church, then became a powerful witness for Christ in the synagogues. Like his Master, he was falsely accused and convicted, but the last sermon he preached cut to the hearts of the listeners. Stephen died revealing glory on his face and seeing Jesus in glory in heaven. Jesus got up from the throne to welcome him! Though he had a glorious entrance into heaven, he was still missed by the church, and the people mourned him (Acts 8:2). It's likely that Stephen's triumphant prayer and death had a great deal to do with preparing Saul's heart for his conversion experience (Acts 22:20). We never know how God will use the death of a believer that to us seems tragic.

Romans 8:28 is still in the Bible, and God is *right now* working all things for His glory and our good.

ACTS 9:32–43. Peter's itinerant ministry took him to Lydda, where God used him to heal a paralytic named Aeneas, and then to Joppa, where Peter raised Dorcas (Tabitha) from the dead. Both miracles resulted in many trusting Christ (vv. 35, 42). People in the local churches, like people in the synagogues, assisted families in the preparation of bodies for burial, and the believers didn't hesitate to display their grief. The burial of the dead is more complex today—or at least we've made it that way—but believers ought to be available to the bereaved to show their love, share their sympathy, and serve in any way they can. It isn't wrong to mourn a lost friend or to honor people for the faithful service they gave to the Lord while they lived. Compare Peter's words and actions here with those of Jesus when He raised Jairus's daughter from the dead (Mark 5:35–43).

ACTS 12. James was the first apostolic martyr. He and his brother John, along with their mother, had asked Jesus for special thrones in the kingdom. The brothers assured the Lord that they could "drink the cup" of suffering that was required (Matthew 20:20–28). Now James had indeed drunk that cup. John lived the longest of the apostles but suffered as an exile on the Isle of Patmos. Why James was slain and Peter miraculously delivered is a question we can't answer. In Acts 1, the church chose a new apostle to replace Judas, but nobody was selected to replace James. Now that the Gentiles were openly a part of the church (Acts 10), there was no need for twelve apostles witnessing to the twelve tribes of Israel in Jerusalem.

We have already considered Peter's death as dealt with in John 21 and 2 Peter 2.

PAUL: FROM THE TRENCHES

Paul wrote his epistles from the trenches, not from a comfortable outpost behind the lines, which means that he knew about suffering, danger, and death from difficult personal experience. At the very beginning of his ministry, Paul was confronted with death as the enemies of the gospel tried to kill him (Acts 9:23–30). "I die every day," he wrote to the Corinthian church, and added "I mean that, brothers" (1 Corinthians 15:31). The mob stoned him in Lystra, but by the grace of God, he got up and went back to work (Acts 14:19–20). Read 2 Corinthians 1:9–11;

4:7–12; 6:3–10; and 11:16–12:20 for insight into what Paul suffered for Jesus Christ; yet through it all, he knew that nothing—not even death—could separate him from Christ's love (Romans 8:35–39). He was willing to go to Jerusalem to die for Christ (Acts 21:13; 25:11), and while a prisoner in Rome, he courageously faced death (Philippians 1:20–21; 2 Timothy 4:7–8). Before his conversion, Paul persecuted Christians "to their death" (Acts 22:4), and the death of Stephen made a great impression on him (Acts 7:54–8:3; 22:20).

It's safe to say that, to Paul, death for the believer was an important event, not just a natural human experience. It was the last opportunity on earth to glorify Christ (Philippians 1:20–21), and he wanted to make the most of it. He wanted to end well.

PAUL AND THE DEATH OF JESUS CHRIST

Paul's life, theology, and ministry were centered in the cross and his personal identification with Christ in death, burial, and resurrection (Ephesians 2:4–10; Romans 6). To Paul, the death of Christ was the greatest expression of God's love (Romans 5:8; Ephesians 5:25). Because of that sacrifice, believers have freedom from the law (Romans 7:4; Galatians 5:1), from sin and condemnation (Romans 5:9; 2 Corinthians 5:21; Colossians 1:19–22), and from death (1 Corinthians 15:50–58).

When Paul wrote his last epistle, he was awaiting a Roman trial and anticipating probable execution, but he rejoiced that Christ had "destroyed death and . . . brought life and immortality to light through the gospel" (2 Timothy 1:10). The word translated "destroyed" means "to nullify, to reduce to inactivity, to disarm." For the believer, death is now "sleep" and we don't mourn or fear as people who have no hope (1 Thessalonians 4:13–18).

PAUL AND THE RESURRECTION OF CHRIST

First Corinthians 15 is the key passage on the resurrection. Some of the people in the Corinthian church did not believe in the resurrection of the human body, even though they did believe in the resurrection of Jesus Christ. In 15:1–19, Paul showed the absurdity of their position, for if there is no resurrection, how could Christ have been raised from the dead? Yet He *was* raised, and Paul proved it! If Jesus has been raised from the dead, and we are identified with Him as members of His body (1 Corinthians 12:27), then we share in His resurrection life. In 15:20–28, Paul used the analogy of the "Last Adam" as he did in Romans 5:12–21 and pointed out that the bodies of the believing dead would be raised in glory at the coming of Christ. (See also 1 Thessalonians 4:13–18.)

In 15:29–34, Paul pointed out that the resurrection wasn't an impersonal or impractical doctrine, for it impacts the daily lives of believers. Salvation involves the whole person, not just the soul or spirit, and what we do with our bodies affects our relationship with God and our ministry to the lost. Are we willing to die for Christ? Are we willing to live for Christ and separate ourselves from the sinful ways of the world? Why? Because one day we shall have glorified bodies and be judged by the Lord. We are "living sacrifices" (Romans 12:1–2), and whether we live or die, we are the Lord's (Romans 14:7–9).

> THE GREEKS THOUGHT THAT RESURRECTION
> WAS IMPOSSIBLE, BUT PAUL POINTED OUT THAT
> NOTHING WAS IMPOSSIBLE WITH GOD.

The Greeks thought that resurrection was impossible (see Acts 17:16–34), but Paul pointed out that nothing was impossible with God (1 Corinthians 15:35–48). Resurrection is not reconstruction. Just as seeds "die" in the ground and produce flowers and fruits, so the dead body is "planted" in the ground and will be transformed into a glorious body at the coming of the Lord. God doesn't "put the pieces together," because the body has been reduced to basic elements that have been redistributed. God gives a new body. There is continuity between the old body and the new (as with the seed and the flower), but there is not identity. It isn't the same body that was buried.

In his epistles, Paul uses three words to describe the deathlessness of the resurrection body: *athanasia,* which means "immortality" (1 Corinthians 15:53–54), and *aphtharsia* and *aphthartos,* which mean "incorruptible, immortal" (1 Corinthians 15:42, 50, 53, 54; 2 Timothy 1:10). The immortal God (1 Timothy 6:16) gives us a new body that cannot die. But keep in mind that the unsaved also receive immortality, but it is "endless death," the second death in the lake of fire (Revelation 20:7–15).

PAUL AND THE RETURN OF CHRIST

Christians today live in the "much mores" of Romans 5, but one day we shall enjoy the "no mores" of Revelation 20–21! Heaven is so wonderful that John couldn't find words to describe what it is, so he told us what it isn't! And Revelation 21:4 is too wonderful for words—"There will be no more death. . . ."

THE CHALLENGE OF PREACHING HEAVEN

It's difficult to preach heaven in the Western world, because we're a society that has everything and takes it all for granted. The church in the West isn't suffering too much, so why talk about the glories of heaven while things seem pretty glorious on earth? What kind of "good news" do we have for affluent people who are enjoying this life and not thinking much about the next life? But Paul and the believers in his day were paying a price to worship Jesus Christ and share His message of life, and the coming of Christ to rescue us and take us to heaven was indeed a blessed hope.

The key passage is 1 Thessalonians 4:13–18, where you find the return of Jesus, the resurrection of the bodies of believers who died whom the Lord brings with Him, the rapture of the living believers, the reunion of both in the air with the Lord, and the rejoicing that we will be "forever with the Lord." Paul saw all of this as a means of encouraging and comforting God's people. Each chapter in 1 Thessalonians ends with a reference to the coming of Christ, and Paul relates Christ's return to practical living: salvation (chapter 1), service (chapter 2), stability (chapter 3), sorrow (chapter 4), and sanctity (chapter 5). See also 1 John 3:1–3.

In the book of Revelation, Jesus has the keys to death and hades (1:18) and will one day see to it that both death and hades are destroyed (20:13–14; 21:4; see 1 Corinthians 15:26). He will put an end to the rider on the pale horse (Revelation 6:7–8). It's too bad that the only time many Christians talk about heaven is when someone they love is dying or has just died, because Jesus saw heaven as a motivation and not just a destination. Trace the phrase "where I am" in the gospel of John and see how Jesus applies going to heaven in a practical way to a bold witness (7:34), true surrender (12:26), an untroubled heart (14:1–6), and the unity of God's people (17:20–24). If we really believe we are going to heaven, we will tell others about Christ, let Him "plant us" where He wants us, not worry about life or death, and promote the unity of the family of God.

THE CHURCH IN THE WEST ISN'T SUFFERING TOO MUCH, SO WHY TALK ABOUT THE GLORIES OF HEAVEN WHILE THINGS SEEM PRETTY GLORIOUS ON EARTH?

"If you read history," wrote C. S. Lewis in *Christian Behavior*, "you will find that the Christians who did the most for the present world were precisely those who thought the most of the next. It is since Christians have largely ceased to think of the other world that they have become so ineffective in this" (Macmillan, 1946; p. 55). D. L. Moody warned about Christians who were "so heavenly minded they were no earthly good," and that must also be avoided. When our lives are motivated by heaven, we will be like Jesus, who endured the cross because of "the joy set before him," the joy of returning to heaven (Hebrews 12:1–2). This also includes the joy of one day presenting His glorious bride to the Father (Jude 24).

It's time that the church said more about death, heaven, and Christ's coming for His people. But let's say it in a practical way that motivates people to holy living and loving care for those who sorrow.

Death and
the Physician

Gathered around the hospital bed, the family waited anxiously. The doctor had moved Hazel into the hospice inpatient unit so she would be more comfortable, but Hazel, now eighty-six years old, had struggled with a heart condition for years, and the end was drawing near. Her breathing grew more labored and shallow. At one point she exhaled but didn't draw another breath for what seemed a long time.

"Is she gone?" asked her son.

Suddenly she took a deep breath and began to breathe normally again. The hospice nurse explained that this was not uncommon as a patient's body shut down. Two hours later, Hazel took her final breath, but the family waited quietly for several minutes, thinking that she might breathe again.

Meanwhile, three blocks away in the critical care unit, another family was watching the husband and father who had suffered severe head trauma in an auto accident. Tests had revealed that Bruce was showing no brain activity. A respirator was doing his breathing, and the steady intravenous drip maintained his blood pressure.

"There's nothing we can do for him," the doctor said. "The machine and the medication are keeping his body alive, but he's already gone."

"How can that be?" demanded Bruce's wife. "His color is good and his breathing is regular. Maybe with time and treatment he can recover."

The doctor said it as gently as possible: "Bruce is brain-dead, and for that there's no treatment. If we disconnect the respirator and stop artificially raising his blood pressure, his body will stop functioning in a very short time. He can't think, and his brain is so badly damaged that it can't keep his body functioning. You and the family must decide how long you want us to continue the respirator and the IV."

"But he looks so alive," whispered Bruce's daughter.

THE DOCTOR'S GROWING INVOLVEMENT

Because more people die in hospitals and other care facilities than at home, and because advanced medical technology is used so extensively, the medical profession has a growing influence on the timing, speed, and nature of the patient's death. It is, therefore, critically important that the pastor or other provider of care understand the physician's role at the end of life—as well as his or her relationship with the patient's family.

The older we become, the more important it is to have a good relationship with our personal physician. Consider these statistics:

- More than 80 percent of Americans die in health care institutions.
- Prior to their death, 25 to 35 percent are in intensive care units.
- 70 to 75 percent die of a chronic illness that lasts about two years.
- 40 to 70 percent needlessly suffer significant pain.
- 25 to 35 percent impose heavy financial obligations on their families.
- 75 percent of the adults are hospitalized sometime the year before they die.
- Almost 60 percent see their doctor five times during their final year of life.[1]

DEATH and the PHYSICIAN

"How Much Time?"

One of the most difficult questions the physician has to answer is, "How much time do I have left?" We recall a doctor who regularly reminded his patients, "I'm a medical doctor, not a witch doctor, so I can't predict the future." Consider this scenario as the doctor speaks to the patient.

"That's the diagnosis, Don. The cancer is inoperable, but we can fight it with radiation and medicine. I can keep you feeling fairly good most of the time, but there will be bad days as well. Please understand, there is no cure, but we can provide a reasonably good quality of life."

Don took his wife's hand. Both of them were crying. "How much time do we have?" she asked.

"I'm not a prophet," he began, "and a lot depends on your attitude, Don, and how your body responds to the treatments. This kind of cancer tends to be slow moving, but there are a lot of variables to consider."

"We understand that," said Don, "but can you give us an idea of what to expect?"

Reluctantly, the doctor replied, "Knowing what I do about your general health and this type of cancer, I'd say six to eighteen months. But we just can't say for sure, so don't take this as final."

Of course, this is a fictional conversation, but it's based on many real conversations and illustrates the dynamics involved in trying to predict life and death.

The doctor clearly stated that the disease was incurable, but he offered hope for the days to come. Patients see their physician as the expert, and they want his help in facing the future. "To predict death is a way to control it."[2] The doctor doesn't want to promise more than he can deliver should the patient die much sooner, nor does he want to be wrong if the patient lives much longer. Despite the doctor's disclaimer, Don and his wife will count on at least eighteen more months together and thus set themselves up for great joy or deep disappointment.

Physicians are expected to be able to provide an accurate timeline for the patient's process of dying, for, after all, life and life's ending are their specialties. Diagnosing a disease is one thing, but predicting its course and when death will occur is not an exact science. Survival depends a great deal on the type of disease or injury, the patient's faith and will to live, the medical procedures used, the support of family and friends, and the quality of relationship between the patient, the family, and the doctor.

THE UNIVERSE OPERATES A DAY AT A TIME,
AND JESUS ADMONISHED HIS DISCIPLES
TO LIVE THE SAME WAY.

This means that the pastor or counselor must approach with "gentle directness" the matter of when death may occur. "Remember, your doctor does not know how long you have" is an honest statement that makes no promises. Patients must be encouraged to trust God, as David did when he wrote, "My times are in Your hand" (Psalm 31:15 NASB). Our future is God's province whether we are healthy or sick, and Christians trust in the loving providence of God (Romans 8:28).

"Yet you do not know what your life will be like tomorrow. You are just a vapor that appears for a little while and then vanishes away. Instead, you ought to say, 'If the Lord wills, we will live and also do this or that'" (James 4:14–15 NASB). The universe operates a day at a time, and Jesus admonished His disciples to live the same way and not fret about tomorrow (Matthew 6:25–34).

DEATH: WHEN THE DOCTOR SAYS SO

When is a person "dead"? How do we define "death"? This is the domain of medicine where the doctors make the decisions. No one is dead until the doctor says so.

Physicians and nurses are trained to help save lives. Death is the enemy; and every victory over death is only temporary, because eventually patients do die. When a patient dies, it means that the treatment failed or that the patient was "too far gone" to be able to respond to the treatment. So we shouldn't be surprised when even medical personnel disagree over the definition of death.

There's a universal agreement that *death is when life ceases,* but it isn't that simple, as our two opening scenarios illustrate. By what criteria do we know that life has ceased? Who established the criteria? (Living people obviously, but how?) Does one definition of death fit all cases and apply in all places? Actually, from the medical point of view there are several kinds of death.

To begin with, there is *clinical death,* when the heart stops beating and the lungs stop breathing. In 1968 the Council of the International Organization of Medical Science identified five elements that must be present in order to declare a person clinically dead: (1) no response to the environment; (2) no reflexes or muscle tone; (3) no spontaneous breathing; (4) a sudden decline in blood pressure; and (5) a flat electroencephalogram (EEG). But more than one patient whose lungs and heart were not working has been revived, so brain function seems to be the key factor in defining death. According to some, *brain death* has occurred when the EEG gives a flat reading. Others believe that, even if there is some brain activity, the person who no longer has "cognitive function" is brain-dead. The Uniform Determination of Death Act defines death as either the irreversible stoppage of heart and lung functions or the failure to function of the brain and brain stem.[3]

It is not the purpose of this book to enter into the complex problems that cluster around life support systems, living wills, and euthanasia, but we must face the fact that our definition of death depends on our understanding of what we think a "person" is. Those who say death has occurred when there is "no cognitive function" are declaring that a person is someone who can interact with the environment and other people. This utilitarian approach could ultimately open the way to involuntary euthanasia, allowing death as a "management option" (Vautier, p. 99). Those who see all human beings as persons, regardless of functional ability, argue for a definition of death demanding that all brain activity has ceased.

Biblically, a human being has both a material body and an immaterial part called the soul and spirit (Genesis 2:7). That sounds dualistic, but persons are more than just the union of the material and the immaterial. There is a living entity that makes persons unique. Is a human being a body animated by a spirit, or is a human being a spirit that is embodied? The answer to both questions is—yes. Death occurs when the soul/spirit leaves the body (James 2:26), and at that point the body begins to decay and return to the dust. From the medical point of view, dying is the process that leads to death, the permanent state. For the

Christian believer, to be absent from the body means to be at home with the Lord (2 Corinthians 5:8).

HOLDING DEATH AT BAY

If doctors who served in the Civil War (1861–1865) could tour a state-of-the-art university hospital today, they would think they had entered the age of miracles. They would marvel at open-heart surgeries, intensive care units, monitored anesthesia, respirators, pacemakers, controlled sterile environments, powerful antibiotics, and a host of other medical procedures and devices that we take for granted. Patients today routinely survive incredible traumas and complex operations and even organ transplants. Physicians and surgeons in the twenty-first century can hold death at bay, at least for a time. Even when a patient can't be cured, doctors can often successfully prolong the life so that the patient can experience some quality of life and have time to prepare for death. It also gives the family opportunity for closure and making plans for the future.

Along with family and medical personnel, there are "invisible people" in that hospital room with the terminally ill or fatally injured patient: hospital administrators, insurance representatives, attorneys (if there's a living will), and perhaps even the press. All of this puts pressure on the family as they are making critical decisions. A doctor may want to try a new procedure or may be worrying because family must be told that there is no hope. The hospital administration might be discussing with the insurance representative the high cost of the patient's care. Their primary question is, "Who will pay the bill?"

If they haven't already conveyed their wishes, many patients get upset because they are being forced to live longer than they can endure, but they can't express themselves clearly. A doctor's refusal to accept the inevitable may put the patient through unnecessary and expensive procedures that only add to his pain.

"Pulling the plug" is an emotionally charged decision. The weight of that solemn responsibility can frighten and overwhelm a patient's spouse, child, or other family members. If a decision must be made, we must rely on the expertise of the doctors—as well as many tears and much prayer. The matter cannot be rushed. Here are some of the questions for careful consideration:

- Are we following what we know are the patient's directives?
- Are we *permitting* death or *causing* death?
- Which is more important, to relieve suffering or prolong life?
- What will be done further if the patient continues to live?
- Are alternative forms of medical care available?
- Are we following medical counsel or personal feelings?

For the Christian, faith in the sovereign will of God gives strength for making these demanding decisions. We have seen patients live a few hours or even days after the family agreed to the removal of life support, and then the patient quietly died. If the Lord chooses to sustain life in such cases, then His will is done; but He always ends life when the right time comes. Job was right when he said, "The Lord gave and the Lord has taken away. Blessed be the name of the Lord" (Job 1:21 NASB). For those prepared to meet their Lord, there is no fear, for the issues of life and death are in His hands (Psalm 139:13–16).

Hastening Death (Euthanasia)

In the Netherlands where it is legally practiced, euthanasia is defined as "the active killing of a patient, at his or her request, by a physician."[4] The state of Oregon approved a Death with Dignity Act in 1994, which was upheld by the U.S. supreme Court in 2006, permitting a physician to write a prescription for a pill or liquid that when ingested will kill the patient. Both of these processes are also called "physician-assisted suicide."

Most physicians resist applying their healing arts for the purpose of ending life. They are trained to save life and not destroy it. But some physicians are willing to assist those who want to die. Some have provided involuntary euthanasia for disabled infants (Vautier, p. 99), and others have increased the dosage of a legal narcotic in order to hasten the patient's death. Once again, the definition of death is a crucial issue. If God is the giver of life, then only He can take it away, and events must run their course. If God has determined the number of our days (Psalms 139:13–16; 39:4), then we cannot go beyond them, *but we can foolishly hasten the day of our death.*

Organizations like hospice don't advocate euthanasia. Their purpose is to make the dying person comfortable, provide care and companionship, and use medicines to alleviate pain but not hasten death. Nobody wants to see a loved one suffer unnecessarily; yet dying is a part of life, and faith tells us that the Lord's purposes are fulfilled even in experiences we can't understand. To end a life prematurely is to play God, something none of us are qualified to do.

LEGAL MATTERS

When patients learn that their condition is terminal, they should provide copies of their living will or medical directives to the attending physician, who will then share them with the hospital staff and any other doctors involved.

When a person dies who is under a doctor's care, the doctor must provide a signed death certificate before the funeral director can take the body and prepare it for burial. If the death results from an accident, homicide, or suicide, the medical examiner will investigate and provide the death certificate.

In most states, the law requires an autopsy in the event the death is unexpected or unexplained: a homicide, a poisoning, an electrocution, an on-the-job fatality, the result of fire, the result of "therapeutic misadventures," a sudden collapse and death in a public place, if it took place during surgery, or if it was the result of gunshot wounds (*Iowa State Handbook for Medical Examiners,* p. 15). The family should be informed of this and is expected to cooperate and plan accordingly. Once the autopsy is completed, the body is released to the funeral home.

When death is from an illness, the family can request an autopsy, especially if the death involved some genetic factor that the survivors should know about and address.

As we minister to patients and interact with medical personnel, it's crucial that we be aware of the issue of confidentiality. The Health Insurance Portability and Accountability Act (HIPAA, 1996) was designed to make sure that workers could retain their health insurance if they changed jobs, but this act also contains definite security guidelines. The only way a spiritual caregiver can get valid information about a patient and the patient's condition is from the patient. If you phone the hospital to see if someone you're seeking is a patient there, the receptionist may not tell you *unless the person indicated at admission that he or she wanted the pastor and church to know.* This is also true of hospital dismissal. No staff member—and this includes the hospital chaplain—is obligated to share information about a patient's whereabouts or medical condition. Before going in for surgery, the patient may want to have the pastor present to pray; but the pastor will probably be asked to enter the room or cubicle at the last minute, lest he or she hear some confidential information that the law doesn't want them to hear.

All of this is for the safety and protection of the patients and the medical personnel, so we must be patient and understanding. Medical personnel want to be helpful, but we must never speak or act in any way that would put them in a compromising situation. Let's play by the rules and not be a part of the problem.

ORGAN AND BODY DONATION

In most states, when you apply for a driver's license or a renewal, you are given the opportunity on the application to donate tissue and organs when you die. In some hospitals, when a death is imminent, the family is asked if they wish to make organ donations. Some of these transplants must be done quickly—heart, lungs, kidneys, and liver—while eyes, corneas, skin, and bones can be donated a few hours after death.

For whatever reasons, not everyone is willing to consider organ donations; but those who do cooperate know that they are contributing to life or improving the quality of life for others. It's estimated that around 400,000 people in the United States are waiting for organ transplants, but there is a shortage of organs. During the 1990s there were over 13,000 people waiting to receive livers, but only 1,549 organs were available.

Some patients arrange to have their body donated to a medical school, and this is especially helpful when their illness has been unique or rare. In some states, the Department of Health can arrange for a body to be donated to science. There are guidelines that must be followed to make sure donations are acceptable, but age is not usually a factor. When the technicians are finished with the body, there is a memorial service held at the school and the remains (or cremains) are returned to the family for burial.

Physicians can overcome disease with medication and surgery, but they cannot defeat death. Patients can follow directions and fight hard, but eventually death will come to all of us, unless the return of the Lord intervenes. As Christian caregivers, our role is to foster a healthy relationship between patient and physician and to clarify questions and seek accurate answers. We also want to sustain and strengthen personal faith in Christ and to remind the patient and the medical team that life and death are in God's hands, but what we do with life and how we face death is up to us.

Notes

1. Nicholas A. Christakis, *Death Foretold: Prophecy and Prognosis in Medical Care* (Chicago and London: University of Chicago Press, 1999), 24.

2. Ibid., 28.

3. John F. Kilner, Arlene B. Millerand, Edmund D. Pellegrino, eds., *Dignity and Dying: A Christian Appraisal* (Grand Rapids: Eerdmans, 1996), 165.

4. Ibid., 96.

Death and the Christian Caregiver

Paul's grandfather had been slowly dying, and the family knew it. Early one Monday, Paul stopped to visit him, greeted his grandmother, and then went to his grandfather's hospital bed in the living room. When Paul took his grandfather's hand, the elderly man opened his eyes and looked at his grandson, who said, "I love you, Grampa." His grandfather smiled, leaned back on the pillow, exhaled, and suddenly was gone. Later Paul asked, "How can somebody be here one second and not here the next second?" Well, it happens, and it's called death.

Megan's best friend, Jan, was killed in an accident caused by a drunk driver. Megan had never been in a funeral home in all her seventeen years, and the mingled fragrances of flowers, cosmetics, and chemicals was disturbing. She waited her turn in line, signed the guest book, spoke to Jan's parents, and then turned to look into the casket. In spite of the patience and skill of the embalmer and the cosmetician, Megan didn't think the girl in the casket looked like Jan. Megan held her breath, turned away from the casket, and ran to the restroom where she threw up. Her first encounter with death was just too much for her.

THE BIBLE: TAKING DEATH SERIOUSLY

Whether we like it or not, everybody must accept the reality of death and learn to come to terms with it, and the earlier this happens in life, the better it will be for the individual. Those of us who minister to the sick, the dying, and those who experience the death of loved ones must know what we believe and why we believe it; otherwise, how can we provide guidance and comfort to those who need it?

We have already covered what the Bible teaches about death and the images it uses to teach us, but now we want to apply this information to the ministry of comforting the bereaved.

People seem to forget that *death is a divine judgment because of the willful disobedience of our first parents* (Genesis 2:16–17; 3:1–19). At the same time, death is a merciful act of God; for if there were no death, corrupt sinners would live forever without hope in decaying bodies surrounded by a deteriorating environment. If there were no death, the Redeemer could not have come to earth as the Last Adam to die for the sins of the world and open the door to everlasting life for those who trust Him.

We die individually, which shows the value of the individual to the Lord. "Precious in the sight of the Lord is the death of His godly ones" (Psalm 116:15 NASB). To God, death isn't cheap or meaningless. It's not an accident; it's an appointment (Hebrews 9:27). God's children have been purchased by the precious blood of His Son (1 Peter 1:18–19) and are very precious to Him. He will not leave to chance their homecoming glory.

But death is a mystery, and we can't be sure when it will take place. Even in a busy hospital, people are quiet and respectful in a room where death has occurred. But, for that matter, *life is a mystery*. The late Dr. Carl Sagan, the popular television lecturer, wrote this about life: "Yet despite the enormous fund of information that . . . biological specialties [have] provided, it is a remarkable fact that no general agreement exists on what it is that is being studied. There is no generally accepted definition of life" (*Encyclopedia Britannica,* 15th edition, vol. 10, p. 893). Despite the reports of people who claim to have had "out-of-body experiences," and apart from the "revelations" of the spiritists, the only certain knowledge we have about the origin and meaning of life and death comes from the Word of God. Jesus Christ is the only person who has died and risen from the dead, never to die again, and who has returned to tell us about it (Revelation 1:4–18).

Death introduces uncertainty into life. "I do not know the day of my death," said Isaac (Genesis 27:2 NASB), and James 4:13–17 admonishes us to remember that life passes swiftly and death often comes unexpectedly. The farmer in our Lord's parable (Luke 12:16–21) had a false sense of security because he ignored this truth. The uncertainties of life and death encourage us to listen to God's Word and live by faith.

> BUT NO MATTER WHERE YOU READ ABOUT
> DEATH IN YOUR BIBLE, YOU LEARN THAT
> THE WRITERS TAKE DEATH SERIOUSLY.

Death is final as far as this world is concerned. When our loved ones leave us, they do not return to us (2 Samuel 12:23). The death of a loved one is like an amputation that never really heals. For Christian believers, the fact of death enhances the reality of heaven and sharpens our anticipation of being there. For unbelievers, all they have is in this life and its transient pleasures. "Let us eat and drink, for tomorrow we die" (1 Corinthians 15:32 NASB). Psalm 90 suggests that the reality of death should remind us of God's sovereignty (v. 3), man's frailty (vv. 4–6), life's brevity (v. 10), the importance of using our time wisely (vv. 12–15), and the necessity of having a purpose in life (vv. 16–17).[1]

Death gives evidence of the reality of sin and the necessity of sinners being born again through faith in Christ. Our time on earth is short, and we must make the best use of our opportunities (Ecclesiastes 9:10) and our possessions (Psalm 49:16–20; Luke 12:13–21). Death is the great leveler—we all return to the dust (Psalm 49:7–10; Ecclesiastes 2:14–18; 8:6–10). Keep in mind that all Old Testament Scriptures about death must be read and interpreted in light of what Jesus revealed and the apostles taught (2 Timothy 1:10). But no matter where you read about death in your Bible, you learn that *the writers take death seriously.* The shadow of death falls across every life, young or old, and even the healthiest and most active.

THE EIGHT STAGES OF GRIEF

Along with our knowledge of the biblical theology of death, we must also have an understanding of the ways people usually respond to the death of a loved one. To understand the "grief process" also means we can interpret our own experience with the sorrowing and more effectively minister to them. Our task is not to shelter people from the pain of grief but to assist them in drawing upon the spiritual resources available through Jesus Christ. They must accept their situation maturely and by the grace of God use it creatively so that they will emerge from the valley better people and stronger Christians.

The people who have studied the psychology of grief tell us that the mourner usually goes through eight stages before coming to acceptance and peace.

1. SHOCK. When the news of a death comes to us, or when we witness the death ourselves, we experience shock, an emotional numbness that is triggered by the body's glandular and nervous systems. This is God's way of temporarily anesthetizing us so we can face the reality of the situation without falling apart. However, sometimes the numbness is so deep that spouses can make all the funeral arrangements and then later not remember the service or some of the friends who spoke to them. If this stage lasts too long, it is abnormal and will create serious problems.

2. STRONG EMOTION. God made us to be able to weep, and tears are always in order when the heart is broken. To tell a grieving person, "Don't cry," is to command her to deny or bury honest emotion instead of expressing that emotion in a normal, healthy response. If the mourning person does bury her emotions, those feelings will later, and inevitably, manifest themselves in unhealthy ways. Abraham wept when his wife, Sarah, died (Genesis 23:2), and Joseph wept when his father died (Genesis 50:1). David was deeply moved and wept when he heard his son Absalom had been slain (2 Samuel 18:33), and the believers in the early church wept when Stephen was martyred (Acts 8:1–2). Our Lord wept when He visited the tomb of His beloved friend Lazarus.

The Bible doesn't tell us it's wrong to express sorrow; what it warns against is sorrowing like the people of the world who have no hope

(1 Thessalonians 4:13–18). Christians can have tears in their eyes while at the same time having joy in their hearts, knowing that their loved one is in heaven with Christ. Some people show their emotions openly and without embarrassment, while others may feel the pain just as deeply but can't easily cry. They may pace from window to window at home, go for walks, or talk endlessly, but this is their way of handling the grief. Others show their grief by expressing anger. The ability to cry and not be ashamed of it is a good thing, and when it's absent, it's a signal for the caregiver to get more involved.

3. DEPRESSION. This is sometimes accompanied by a smothering feeling of loneliness and perhaps by physical problems such as headaches, sleeplessness or sleeping too much, or loss of appetite or eating too much. Depressed people often take little interest in the normal activities of life and have a hard time making simple decisions. All of life becomes very gloomy. But when you consider that the death of a loved one often means that deep relationships have been broken and that life must be completely reorganized, is there any wonder that people become depressed? If these symptoms persist, it may be necessary to call in professional help. Grief has its time (Ecclesiastes 3:4), and if that time extends longer than necessary, something is wrong and intervention is needed.

4. FEAR. It's frequently difficult for grieving persons to concentrate and make decisions, and this can create fear and even panic. They feel like life is falling apart both within them and around them. They are afraid to be alone; they fear they will forget their departed loved one; they fear they will lose their sanity and that life will always be this way. If the loved one died in a car accident, they may develop a fear of driving or riding in a vehicle. If the deceased person died from disease, the mourner may develop a morbid fear of germs or hospitals or even doctors. The grieving person's biggest fear is that life will never be normal again. Of course, in many respects life cannot be the same again, but the bereaved person can learn to make adjustments. These people need to be lovingly reassured that they will gradually heal, get a new perspective, and return to life with its duties and delights.

5. GUILT. Grieving people may start taking the blame for the death of their loved one, and this guilt is compounded if the death was a suicide. Grief opens up old wounds and memories. There is also a tendency for mourners to idealize the deceased person and magnify the good points to the exclusion of the truth. Guilt often leads to a bad case of the "if onlys"—"If only I had called the doctor sooner," "If only we hadn't let him take the car," "If only we had chosen a different highway." (See John 11:21, 32.) A temporary case of the "if onlys" can be a normal grief response, but the maintaining of a false guilt about something beyond their control is a sign of a deeper problem that must be addressed. Some people *want* to take the blame; it's a form of penance. True guilt can be forgiven through confessing the sin to the Lord and claiming His promised forgiveness (1 John 1:9), but false guilt must be confronted in a gentle but firm way.

6. ANGER. Along with blaming themselves, grieving people may also blame other people, including the deceased loved one. When a wife asks, "Why did he have to leave me and the children now?" she's voicing her frustration at having to accept all the burdens without being given a choice. Perhaps she's justified in being angry at her husband's absence, but that isn't the same as being angry at her husband, unless his death was the result of his own folly. Used in a mature way, anger is one of the most powerful of the defense mechanisms. It can help relieve tension, or it can create even more tension. Anger is our response to a real or imagined threat, and it may bring people closer to us or keep them at a greater distance so they can't hurt us again. Feelings of guilt and anger, hidden or expressed, can fuel painful disagreements among families during times of bereavement. Death not only *creates* problems, but it also *reveals* them. The feeling of helplessness that often accompanies bereavement can lead to anger—or to apathy.

DEATH NOT ONLY *CREATES* PROBLEMS,

BUT IT ALSO *REVEALS* THEM.

7. APATHY. It seems strange that hostility can lead to apathy and withdrawal, but this is often the case. The storm is followed by a dangerous calm. The usual evidence of this stage is the repeated statement, "Nobody understands how I feel"; and since the person really believes this, nobody can explain anything or take any action to help. Of course, many people *have* experienced the pain of bereavement and can empathize, but it's a waste of time to argue the point. "Life just isn't worth living" is often the next evidence of apathy. The bereaved person has a hard time relating to the situation and to other people, and this makes it easier to withdraw into his or her own world and fight the battle alone—or stop fighting altogether.

In every life there's a need for solitude but never for estrangement and alienation. Solitude gives us strength to return to society and build bridges, but isolation only builds walls. Family and friends must encourage the apathetic person to be a part of the family circle, to get out of the house occasionally, to gradually restore the normal routine. It may take time, but it must be done. Protracted physical and emotional isolation is a signal for special help.

8. *ADJUSTMENT*. Assisted by faith, family, friends, and the normal human abilities and strengths God has given them, grieving people can eventually come to terms with their losses, accept them, and learn to rearrange life to fit reality. What life does *to* us depends largely on what life finds *in* us, and that's where faith in Jesus Christ comes in. Reaching this new level of life doesn't rule out tears, loneliness, or sadness, but it does mean the person now recognizes what's happening and chooses to cope rather than to quit. People die, but relationships never die, even if they exist only in our memories, and the mature person learns to adjust to this new relationship.

One of the first signs of recovery is the person's ability to speak about the deceased person and even remember things to laugh about. At first this may lead to a few tears, but the tears are under control. Another evidence of recovery is positive planning for the future and admitting that life is good. There may still be hours and perhaps days of distress, but the person recognizes the feelings and deals with them. When they can laugh again, when their anger is under control, and when they think more and more about others and less about themselves, they know they are healing.

Not every bereaved person may go through all of these eight stages, or if they do, it might not be in this particular order; but these eight stages are "mileposts" by which the mourners and the caregivers may measure the progress of the journey. Some persons may cycle between two or three stages for a time before moving on, and we need to recognize where they are if we are to bring comfort.

Each of us grieves in different ways and at our own pace, and studies indicate that women and men have different "styles" of grieving. So do teenagers and children. The family (and church fellowship) that encourages open conversation and the healthy expression of emotion will stay closely bonded and provide a loving atmosphere in which grief can do its work in its own time and bring about healing. It's especially important that wives and husbands and parents and children respect each other's "emotional cycles" and not criticize or condemn. God has ordained that we cannot heal our own broken heart; we need the help of others, and they need our help.

Most of the normal stages of healthy grief can become abnormal if taken to excess. Abnormal grief can lead to expressions of violent anger, threats of suicide, and even loss of self-control. Apathy that leads to isolation and the avoidance of human contact is preparing the way for serious problems and requires intentional intervention. Before or after the funeral, the minister may find himself or herself functioning as referee at a family feud, and it's important to remain calm and neutral and seek to be an "instrument of God's peace." We must listen to feelings as well as to words; we should help people identify the real issues; and we must seek to calm ruffled feelings and refocus people who have temporarily lost their perspective.

The British poet and essayist Samuel Johnson said, "Grief has its time. While grief is fresh, every attempt to divert it only irritates. You must wait 'til grief be *digested*." God can heal the brokenhearted, but we must give all the pieces to Him.

ANSWERING THE BIG QUESTIONS

"Where was God when my child died?" is a typical question and a normal one. When asked in a hostile manner, the person is implying that God was not paying attention and therefore permitted an unnecessary death to occur. The questioner is probing for assurance that God hasn't stopped loving them. Sometimes the question means, "I want to wake up and discover that all of this is a dream." A lecture on theology—the mysteries of God's providence, for example—really won't meet the need. *God's people live on promises and not explanations, so refer the hurting person to the great promises of God.* On more than one occasion, we've answered

this question by quietly and lovingly saying, "God was the same place He was when His own Son died—on the throne of heaven, and that's where He is now. Let's trust Him."

"Why did God permit this to happen?" More than one person in Scripture has cried out "Why?" including our Savior when He was dying on the cross. He did it to fulfill the Scriptures, but most people who ask this question think that tragedy is not a part of human life and especially not a part of the dedicated Christian life. But ever since the fall of Adam, tragedy has been inextricably interwoven with human experience. It's unfortunate that the "health and wealth" media preachers have convinced people that faith and obedience will protect people from pain and tragedy, when Scripture teaches just the opposite. Again, a philosophical or theological discussion won't solve the problem, so focus on the promises of God and the reality of the normal Christian life.

"How can God expect me to trust Him when He's permitted this to happen?" This reveals an impulsive heart that wants to believe and be faithful but is shattered by pain. Answering the question may be part of post-funeral counseling when you and the questioner have more time. The writer of Psalm 73 struggled with a similar problem, and so did the prophet Habakkuk. True faith doesn't bargain with God and say, "I'll trust You on my terms." True faith says with Job, "Though He slay me, I will hope in Him" (Job 13:15 NASB). The three friends of Daniel had it right when they told the king, "Our God whom we serve is able to deliver us from the furnace of blazing fire. . . . But even if He does not, let it be known to you, O king, that we are not going to serve your gods or worship the golden image that you have set up" (Daniel 3:17–18 NASB). No bargaining here! God can be trusted no matter what He permits to happen, because He loves us too much to harm us, and He's too wise to make a mistake.

"What's the point of all this pain?" is another version of the previous question. We want life to be orderly and free of pain, but this view of life—at least the Christian life—is badly twisted. What's the point of the Christian life? To become "conformed to the image of His Son" (Romans 8:28–29 NASB). To become more like Jesus involves a certain amount of suffering, for we take up our cross to follow Him. The writer of Psalm 88 is an emotional twin of this questioner.

It's a hopeful sign when people ask questions, because it shows they are thinking and are making an effort to stay connected with reality, even if their views of reality don't have a biblical basis. Wise caregivers accept their feelings expressed and gently answer the *need* and not the *question*. They don't argue or lecture. There are many questions we can't answer, and even if we could, the answer might not meet the real need. We don't know why God permits the tragedies that come to the lives of some of God's choicest people, nor do we need to know. But we do know that He is working for our good (Romans 8:28), that Jesus loves us as much as the Father loves Him (John 15:9), and that the Father loves us as much as He loves Jesus (John 17:23). What more do we need?

SHARE A PROMISE FROM THE WORD,

NOT AS A SERMON TEXT BUT AS

MEDICINE FOR A HURTING HEART.

There are two appropriate responses to those questions that don't have answers. One is, "I don't know the answer, and I don't know anybody who does." The second is, "I don't know the answer, but I do know a promise that can help us deal with the situation." Then share a promise from the Word, not as the text of a sermon but as medicine for a hurting heart. In the throes of grief, when people are desperately trying to make sense out of their painful situation, they may express hostility and even blasphemy against God, or make statements that are bizarre theologically. Listen, love, accept, keep your eye contact, tell them you have heard them, and trust the Spirit of God to work through you to affirm the presence of the Lord at this difficult time. There will be time later to wrestle with theological questions. Right now, it's time to hug—and to weep together.

'REMEMBER YOU ARE DUST'

Worshipers hear those words on Ash Wednesday when the minister imposes the ashes and quotes from the *Book of Common Prayer*, "Remember that you are dust, and to dust you shall return." Moses recorded those words in Genesis 3:19, and God spoke them to Adam and Eve after their disobedience. They remind us that we are mortal, and even the wedding vows include the words "till death us do part." But human beings, including Christian believers, need repeated reminders that life is fragile and, unless our Lord returns, that death is inevitable.

> IT'S POSSIBLE TO GRIEVE OVER THE
> DEATH OF ANOTHER PERSON AND
> NEVER ONCE CONSIDER THAT WE
> MIGHT BE THE NEXT ONE TO DIE.

We ministers assume that the people who attend funerals pay close attention and are keenly aware of the reality of death and the possibility of their own decease. But we are probably wrong. It's possible to grieve over the death of another person *and never once consider that we might be the next one to die.* If they think about it at all, most men and women, and especially teens and children, believe that death is what happens to other people. We are only spectators at funerals; we will never be the center of attention.

This means that we ministers must not limit our teaching about death only to the occasional funeral sermon. The weekly sermon is an unparalleled opportunity for biblical instruction about death as well as life, mortality as well as immortality. "The pastor's care for the dying begins not merely when serious illness occurs," writes Thomas C. Oden, "but long before then, in assisting persons to reflect and meditate on their own vulnerability and mortality."[2] The very message of the gospel involves death—"Christ died for our sins." We should not harp on the theme of death, but neither should we avoid it.

Statistics alone tell us that people need to prepare for death now. Every day, 1,500 Americans die of cardiac ischemia (blocked blood flow), and half of all deaths in the United States involve problems with coronary arteries.[3] The daily news reports seem to focus on death. Who would think that teenage students (and even younger ones) would take a gun to school and shoot teachers and other students? What driver expected to be killed turning from the highway into a supermarket parking lot? Who expects that a loved one will die in surgery, even under the hands of a competent surgeon? The conclusion of the matter: live each day for the Lord as if it will be your last.

The reality of death is related to many basic biblical truths, so it's not too easy to avoid it as we expound the Scriptures, even texts that don't directly relate to physical death. Paul declared to the saints that "the wages of sin is death" (Romans 6:23), a statement that stands at the end of a chapter on the sanctified life of victory. "For this reason many among you are weak and sick, and a number sleep [have died]" (1 Corinthians 11:30 NASB) was written to believers who were abusing the celebration of the Lord's Supper (Eucharist), so the theme of death can even invade the worship service. The unpopular subject of stewardship involves the even more unpopular subject of death, for how we use our resources today will determine how rich we will be in heaven after we die (Matthew 6:22–34) and how many will greet us when we get there (Luke 16:1–15).

As preachers, we need to expose what is false as well as expound what is true, and as we pointed out in chapter 1, we live in a culture that denies death. The very use of everyday language causes people to ignore death. Agents sell people "life insurance," but it's really "death insurance" so the survivors can pay for the funeral. (This is not a criticism of the insurance industry or of the need for insurance.) The unwholesome emphasis on sex is a deliberate attempt to repress the awareness of mortality. If we are teaching our people what is going on in "the world" (1 John 2:15–17), we will have to talk about the reality of death.

The reality of death also brings with it many practical considerations. Many churches sponsor seminars that deal with preparing a will, preparing a living will, planning the funeral, estate planning, caring for the bereaved, and other allied topics, and they bring in experts to lead them. The hospice staff people are excellent sources of information, and so are local funeral directors. Nobody comes to sell anything or buttonhole potential customers. Everybody presents his or her expertise in order to educate Christians about the practical facts of death. If we are to be effective caregivers, we must overcome this careless use of language and speak the truth in love.

TEN COMMANDMENTS FOR CAREGIVERS

When death occurs in a family, immediately go to see them.

Do a great deal of listening. Allow people to express their thoughts and feelings without instantly correcting their bad theology or rebuking their bad attitudes.

Emphasize the promises of God and the unchanging love of God.

Leave the mysteries of life and death unexplained. Be willing to say, "I don't know."

"Weep with those who weep" (Romans 12:15 NASB), but avoid saying, "I know just how you feel." They don't think you do.

Never underestimate the powerful ministry of presence. Simply being there often means more than what we say or do.

Allow mourners to grieve in their own way, at their own pace.

Remind yourself that grieving is a complex process that requires time.

Stay in touch with those who mourn. Let them know you are available.

Keep confidential what you see and hear in private. Don't turn the experience into a sermon illustration, at least not without proper permission.

"Blessed are those who mourn, for they will be comforted."
—JESUS *(Matthew 5:4)*

Notes

1. Moses wrote Psalm 90 as a response to God's judgment of Israel at Kadesh Barnea and must be read in that light (Numbers 13–14). Moses gave us the other side of the coin in Psalm 91.

2. Thomas C. Oden, *Classic Pastoral Care*, vol. 4 (Grand Rapids: Baker, 1994), 164.

3. Sherwin Nuland, *How We Die: Reflections on Life's Final Chapter* (New York: Knopf, 1994), 19, 23.

Death and the Funeral Director

Anyone who has visited the Egyptian wing of a good museum knows that embalming is an ancient practice of which the Egyptians were the recognized masters. According to the Egyptian religion, the proper preparation of the body was important to the well-being of the deceased in the next world, and therefore embalming was as much a religious rite as a sanitary procedure. However, most ancient peoples did not embalm their dead, and this included the Jews. As noted earlier in this book, the Jewish family and/or friends simply washed the corpse, dressed it or wrapped it in cloths, placed it in a simple container (optional), and buried it in the earth or placed it in the family tomb, often a cave. Some ancient peoples cremated dead bodies, and a few exposed their dead to the elements and allowed the carrion-eating birds to take over—something that would be the depth of humiliation for a Jew. For the most part, however, the usual procedure in the ancient world was burial (interment) with or without embalming, and this is the general practice in the Western world today, although more people than before are now opting for cremation. However, even with cremation, the body is usually embalmed.

THE EMERGENCE OF THE FUNERAL DIRECTOR

It surprises many people to learn that the practice of embalming and the profession of the undertaker are relatively new customs in Western society. In the Middle Ages, abandoned (or stolen) corpses were sold to medical schools where they were embalmed and kept for students to study, but most corpses were prepared by the family and buried as quickly as possible, usually with the blessing of the church. This was true in American colonial times and up to the Civil War era.

The embalming process consists of making an incision in an artery, draining the blood from the body, pumping embalming fluid into the body, and stitching the incision. Fluid is also removed from body cavities and replaced with preservatives. If the body has suffered violence, the embalmer may have to invest many hours piecing parts together, stitching and cosmetizing. This is done, not to make the deceased look "alive," but to make them more presentable when family and friends come for that final good-bye.

The embalmer grew in importance during the Civil War, which was the first American war in which the dead (Union dead, for the most part) were embalmed and shipped home for burial. The body of assassinated President Abraham Lincoln was embalmed so it could be carried by train from the nation's capital to his home in Springfield, Illinois, and this event helped to increase the importance of the embalmer in the public eye. In recent years, the work of the funeral director was somewhat enhanced during the events that immediately followed the assassination of President John F. Kennedy, even though the family and the Secret Service had their problems with funeral directors. Kennedy biographer William Manchester tells the story in his *Death of a President.*

Other factors contributed to the development of what some people now call "the deathcare industry."[1] The urbanization of the United States meant that many families lived in smaller quarters and funerals could no longer be conducted in homes. City authorities also established regulations that sought to standardize the registering of deaths, the conducting of viewing and wakes, and the final burial of the body. The hospital, not the home, became the place where most people died, and it was necessary to have the professional services of qualified people to pick up the body and deliver it to the place of embalming.

This led to the development of the "funeral home."

In time, "embalmers" became "undertakers" who in turn became "funeral directors" and then "morticians." An item in *The Literary Digest* of January 16, 1915, announced that "the word 'mortician' is a recent innovation due to a need felt by undertakers for a word more in keeping with, and descriptive of, their calling."[2] The American funeral directors held their first national meeting in 1882; by 1890 there were 9,891 of them and over 24,000 in 1920. By 1934, they were calling their schools "colleges of mortuary science," although their graduates did not receive baccalaureate degrees. Students were taught not only how to prepare the body for viewing and for burial, but also how to provide assistance in planning the funeral service and giving encouragement to the mourners. The new field of "grief therapy" slowly developed. The funeral home was designed to be a place for the displaying of the deceased, the gathering of family and friends, and the conducting of the funeral service. In time, fewer and fewer services were held in homes and churches. The funeral director was expected to provide the family with transportation to and from the cemetery and to give whatever assistance they needed for the official business connected with the death and the burial. "The success of the funeral industry was a product of the radically changing conditions of modern life, and modern dying, in this historical period."[3]

ACCUSATIONS, TRUE AND FALSE

People in the "deathcare industry" have sought to upgrade their schools, equipment, and services, and especially their professional image, and for the most part they have succeeded. Your experience may be different, but we can sincerely say that the funeral directors we've worked with over many years of ministry have appeared to be ethical and professional in every way, and we don't know that any of our people have issued any formal complaints against them. But every profession has its unethical practitioners, and the sins of a few shouldn't make us condemn an entire profession. Not every used-car salesman is a con artist, nor is every mortician out to rob people at a time when their grief makes them vulnerable and easily influenced. The average family has to deal with death only once every fifteen years, and most people are unprepared for the decisions they must make. They find the caring funeral director to be a helpful friend.

But there have been serious accusations against the "deathcare industry," especially the 1963 best seller *The American Way of Death* by Jessica Mitford. While revising her book, Jessica Mitford died in 1986, but her husband completed the updated edition, and it was published in 1988 as *The American Way of Death Revisited* (Alfred Knopf). The purpose of the book didn't change: it still accuses "the undertaking industry" of taking advantage of grieving people, inflating prices, and perpetuating a form of funeral that is "body centered" and expensive. She was able to document a number of customer horror stories that could probably be duplicated in almost any other profession, including law, medicine, finance, and the ministry. As we said before, every profession has its share of unethical people, but in order to have the counterfeit, there has to be the authentic for them to imitate, so why not focus on the genuine practitioners?

In chapter 8 we will discuss the theology and psychology of the funeral service, but since we are examining Jessica Mitford's book, we must deal with some related matters here. Let's begin with the common accusation that funerals are too "body centered." *But the body is all that we have once a loved one has died.* The Lord God buried His servant Moses in a private service on Mount Nebo (Deuteronomy 34), and the body of our Savior was tenderly buried by Joseph and Nicodemus (John 19:38–42). The believers in the Jerusalem church buried Stephen and were not afraid to show their grief (Acts 7:54–8:2). Granted, perhaps too many funerals focus on the dead body and not the life of the deceased, but even this is changing. More and more people are opting for one evening of visitation, a private burial with a brief graveside service, and then a public memorial service where the emphasis is on the celebration of life. Even at traditional funerals, the closed casket is becoming the norm.

EVERY SOCIETY THAT ANTHROPOLOGISTS
HAVE STUDIED HAS HAD SOME KIND
OF RITUAL FOR BIDDING FAREWELL TO THE DEAD.

We might add that the focus of attention at a formal wedding is on bodies—a beautiful bride, a handsome groom, and their attendants—

and many weddings cost more than the average adult funeral, which Mitford says is $7,800, including the burial plot and other cemetery costs. We live in a society that demands that dead bodies be disposed of in an acceptable manner, and rightly so; and surveys indicate that across the country, funeral services are fairly standard. The funeral director prepares the body, not so that people will pretend that the deceased "looks alive," but so that the living may relate to the deceased in a more positive way.

> THE 9/11 TWIN TOWERS TRAGEDY REMINDED
> US THAT PEOPLE WHO HAVE NO TANGIBLE
> REMAINS TO SEE MAY EXPERIENCE NO 'CLOSURE'
> AND SUFFER PROLONGED EMOTIONAL PAIN.

Every society that anthropologists have studied has had some kind of ritual for bidding farewell to the dead. The Christian life has its physical aspects—even our Lord took upon Himself a body so He could do His Father's will—so let's not become super-spiritual and discount the importance of the human body in life or in death. We are not Gnostics. Human families celebrate birth, birthdays, coming-of-age milestones, marriages, personal achievements, and retirements, so why not recognize that final milestone and honor the one we loved and will miss? The 9/11 Twin Towers tragedy has reminded us that people who have no tangible remains to see may experience no "closure" and suffer prolonged emotional pain. "When last rites go wrong, a sense of sacrilege is felt by all, even the irreligious."[4] As we shall see in chapter 8, the proper funeral service can assist the mourners in facing the death honestly, accepting the loss, and taking the first steps toward healing.

THE HIGH COST OF DYING

We sometimes forget that the average funeral director has invested a great deal of money into training, real estate, and equipment, including expensive automobiles, and he certainly can't afford to donate his services.

According to Thomas Lynch, there are 22,000 funeral homes in the United States, and 85 percent of them are still family owned and managed.[5] Like anybody else, if these people don't pay their bills, they go out of business. Many funeral directors have sacrificially served families that were unable to pay them, and perhaps only the county health department knew about it. Some morticians have a policy of giving free burial services to infants, as well as to men and women in the police and fire departments who are killed in the line of duty.

As caregivers, we don't interfere with the financial aspects of funerals unless (1) we are asked our opinion or (2) it's obvious that the people in charge are making unwise decisions that will create serious problems later on. If the deceased left explicit directions concerning interment and the funeral service, they should be followed as much as possible. Professional costs do accelerate, inflation is always at work, and even a prepaid funeral might not provide adequate funds.

One of the most difficult problems is the grieving spouse or parent who wants to devote his or her life savings to the burial of their loved one. Whatever the motive, known or unknown—genuine but misguided love, guilt and atonement, keeping up appearances—the decision is a bad one. Bereavement sometimes knows no logic, so you may not be able to reason with them successfully, but this is the time to work with the mortician and guide the mourner into calmer and safer waters. Most cemeteries today don't permit lavish monuments but instead mark the graves with bronze tablets. We recall one widow who would have sold her home to get "the best" for her husband, but her pastor, the funeral director, and the Lord helped her make a wiser decision.

QUESTIONS FAMILY MEMBERS MAY ASK YOU

The average person experiences a death in the family once in fifteen years, so many people aren't conversant with policies and procedures.

"Where will they take the body?" If the deceased had a prearranged burial plan, the body will go to the funeral home selected, and all the family member in charge has to do is phone the funeral director. If there is no burial plan, the family will have to get together and select a funeral home. The body can remain in hospice a few hours but then must be moved. If the person died in the hospital, it's best to remove the body as

soon as possible, even if temporarily to the hospital morgue or the city or county morgue. There will be a charge for this service.

"What about clothes for the body for the funeral?" The deceased may have already made this choice and informed a family member. The outfit should be complete, including undergarments, hose, and shoes. Don't forget spectacles and dentures.

"How will they style her hair?" Provide the funeral director with a recent photo of the deceased, and a hairdresser will seek to style it accordingly. The ravages of disease, or the consequences of trauma may cause some disfigurement, but you can be sure the funeral home staff will do their best. The family will be asked to view the body at the funeral home before people arrive for the wake, and then you can evaluate the cosmetic work and perhaps make suggestions.

"Must there be an autopsy?" Not unless the family requests it or the law requires it. (See chapter 4, "Legal Matters.") If there's a possibility that genetic factors were involved in the death, the family will want to get as much information as possible.

"What about the death certificate?" The funeral director will provide as many copies as you need for insurance companies, the Social Security Administration, the employer, the military, and any other offices that owe you death benefits.

"Who writes the obituary?" Again, the funeral director will assist the family in doing this. Some local newspapers print a free obituary containing the basic data, but at a reasonable cost they are willing to expand it to include other information. The expanded version is a good opportunity for Christians to share their faith in Christ. If there are family members living at a distance who want their friends to know about the funeral, the local editors can contact newspapers in those areas and provide the facts. Of course, there is a charge for this service.

"What about military honors?" If the deceased has served in the armed forces, share the discharge papers with the funeral director, who will then notify a local veterans' organization to provide an honor guard. The guard will be in uniform and will provide a rifle salute and the playing of taps (often on tape), and will give an American flag to the family. This is done after the graveside committal service. The number of World War II veterans is declining quickly, and therefore in some communities it's becoming difficult to provide traditional honors. The military honors are both

heartwarming and haunting and should be provided if at all possible.

"How do we secure a cemetery plot?" If there is already a family plot where the deceased expected to be buried, the funeral director will notify the cemetery, and the grave will be opened in time for the graveside service and the interment. If a plot must be purchased, a representative from the cemetery will help you decide. The cost of the plot plus the fees for opening and closing the grave will be included in the final statement from the funeral home. Be aware that some cemeteries charge an annual "grounds maintenance fee" and that many cemeteries do not permit headstones or ornate grave decorations. They will sell you a suitable metal marker, and U.S. military branches will provide free a flat marker for veterans. If headstones are permitted, your funeral director will provide you with the locations and phone numbers of monument dealers.

"Must we have a vault for the casket?" The answer depends on state and local laws and cemetery policies. In the old days of wooden coffins, the lids would eventually collapse and cause the surface of the grave to sink. Today's metal caskets are much better constructed, so this isn't likely to occur. But most cemeteries require the casket to be placed in an approved vault to maintain a uniform level to the ground and to avoid unforeseen problems that could threaten the casket and its contents.

"How do we choose a casket?" If the funeral was prepaid, the choice, or at least the price range, has already been decided. If you must make a choice, a funeral home staff member will show you their display room where the prices of the various caskets are clearly seen, and will explain the features of the merchandise. Professional ethics demands that mortuary personnel not take advantage of customers at a time when they are grieving and may be emotionally upset. As we mentioned earlier in this chapter, the casket should be chosen that best fits the family budget and best communicates the character and reputation of the deceased.

"Who orders the flowers?" Most funeral homes will do this for you if you tell them what you want and define the price range. A spray of flowers on the casket from the family is usually sufficient, although individual family members may want smaller floral displays from nieces and nephews, grandchildren, etc. If the funeral home orders the flowers, the cost will be on the final bill. If family members want to take the time to visit the florists, there's nothing to prevent them.

"Do we need funeral coaches for the cemetery procession?" Except for the

hearse and perhaps a flower car, you may use your own cars. In the case of a large family or bad weather, there is something to be said for automotive togetherness, but remember that you will be charged.

"What should we pay the pastor, musicians, and other people who serve?" Local custom and church policy usually govern this. Most pastors don't charge for their ministry, because they expect to serve the people who are members of the church. People outside the church family ought to contribute something to the church in return for their pastor's services to a nonmember. Ministering to the bereaved and conducting funerals will require a great deal of extra time and work, and an honorarium would not be out of order. Some pastors graciously receive such gifts and put them into the church memorial fund or missions fund. We think it's gracious of the family of the deceased to remember the musicians and the church custodian, if the service is held in church facilities. Ask the funeral director for his counsel. He knows the local churches and customs.

BE AT YOUR BEST

If you minister long enough in a community, you get to know the various funeral directors and their associates, and this is helpful to your ministry. But whenever you meet them casually or work with them professionally, always be at your best, and never lower the bar. Let's so live and serve that the way we act doesn't nullify the messages we preach.

A SERMON DOESN'T HAVE TO BE

ETERNAL TO BE IMMORTAL.

Be sure to get the funeral data correct, and *arrive early for the service!* Also, keep your eye on the clock during the service, particularly if another funeral is scheduled at that home. A sermon doesn't have to be eternal to be immortal. Work with the funeral director to help expedite things " decently and in order," and both of you will succeed.

Before the funeral service begins, you ought to be with the family, so don't joke around in the office while drinking free coffee. No matter where we are or who is with us, we must keep our conversation on a high level at all times, and that includes while driving to the cemetery in a funeral home limousine. It's possible to be serious and not somber, grave but not gloomy, friendly but not chummy. From God's point of view, wherever we are, we are on holy ground, so let's always act like dedicated servants of God. If we walk with the Shepherd, we will know what to say and do.

We've learned that competent funeral directors can usually help us better understand the people we are serving, particularly if they have served the family before, but we must never pry and must always keep confidence. A death in the family brings out the best in some people and the worst in others, and we must seek to love and serve them all.

Don't get in the way of the funeral director, but work with him as a fellow caregiver, and seek to share the love of God.

Notes

1. See William Safire's "On Language" column in the *New York Times Magazine* for July 9, 2000, p. 20.

2. See *The Oxford English Dictionary* under "mortician."

3. Gary Laderman, *Rest in Peace: A Cultural History of Death and the Funeral Home in Twentieth-Century America* (New York: Oxford University Press, 2003), 4.

4. "Why Disposing of the Dead Matters to the Living," *New York Times,* February 24, 2002, "The Week in Review" section.

5. *Bodies in Motion and At Rest* (New York: Norton, 2000), 173.

Death and the Family: The Pastoral Opportunity

The phone rang. Pastor Walsh put down his book and said, "Yes?"

"Pastor, the Clark family just called," his assistant said. "Naomi's mother has only a short time to live. They would appreciate it if you could meet them at hospice."

"Can't Larry go? He's the visitation pastor."

"He was already there this morning, and he was also there last night. The Clarks really want to see you."

"I'm the senior pastor, and I don't do visitation!" said Pastor Walsh. "If I did it for one, I'd have to do it for all." He hung up and reached for his book.

Pastor Mike and Cindy were enjoying lunch together at their favorite sandwich shop, a treat that didn't come very often. Mike's cell phone rang just as the waitress brought their dessert.

"This is Barb at the church. You wanted to know when Tom Meier's family got to the hospital. They are there now. Tom is still unresponsive, and they have some big decisions to make."

"Thanks," said Mike. "We're on our way."

"Please package the dessert," Cindy said to the waitress, and they paid the bill and headed for the hospital.

"When It Is Not Convenient"

When death begins to cast its shadow, the Christian caregiver—that is, a member of the pastoral staff, elder, chaplain, or other person responsible for caregiving in the church—is given many opportunities to communicate God's love and truth. Suffering people call for the minister or the chaplain because these set-apart servants represent the Lord and His church, and people in crisis need God's special help. All of which says, *we must be available.* "Be prepared in season and out of season," Paul admonished Timothy (2 Timothy 4:2), which the Berkeley New Testament translates "be at it when it is and when it is not convenient." The question is never, "Do you want me to call?" but "When would you like me to come?"

Even if a family member says, "Oh, Pastor, you don't have to come!" the compassionate shepherd will answer, "Unless it's inconvenient for you, I would like to be there." People remember our kindness and personal ministry long after they forget our wonderful sermons. The presence of the pastor reinforces God's love for hurting people and makes that love real to them. We earn the right to be heard in public when we have demonstrated compassionate care in private.

PEOPLE REMEMBER OUR KINDNESS AND
PERSONAL MINISTRY LONG AFTER THEY
FORGET OUR WONDERFUL SERMONS.

Every family situation is different. No two people in a family respond the same way to the fact of death or the news of death. Some people you thought had deep faith may fall apart, while others you considered less mature will rise to the occasion. Make no permanent evaluations from a crisis situation, but at the same time, don't be fooled by appearances. Since death is an infrequent visitor in most American homes today, this will be a whole new experience for some of the family members. Let them know it's acceptable to cry, that real men shed tears, and that it's normal for children to be disturbed and even frightened. You don't "take over" the household, but your quiet presence, your use of Scripture, and your prayers help to make a difference.

Perhaps the key word is *reassurance*. Shocked and grieving people need to know that God is still on the throne, that they haven't lost control of life no matter how they feel, and that in the course of time they will live balanced lives again. Encourage them to make one decision at a time, to live a day at a time and trust the Lord for guidance. Grief is God's gift to hurting people to help them heal, and this takes time—and this in itself can be difficult for many to deal with. People have unrealistic expectations when it comes to confronting death and sorrow. They may have to learn the hard way; but you will be there to help.

What about the funeral itself? Once the funeral home has the body, the pastor chats with the family about the funeral arrangements. They may have already talked it over—and we must do all we can to fit into their plans. The minister finds out when the family will be going to the funeral home to view the body and plans to arrive before them to meet them at the door and stand with them when they first see their loved one's remains. They may want to pause for prayer before entering the chapel. Remember that it isn't our clever conversation or our extemporaneous sermonettes that assures them of God's care; it's our quiet presence with them and our availability to listen and to serve.

WE EARN THE RIGHT TO BE HEARD
IN PUBLIC WHEN WE HAVE DEMONSTRATED
COMPASSIONATE CARE IN PRIVATE.

MAKING CHRIST REAL IN THE VALLEY OF THE SHADOW

Before we look at ministering to the grieving after the loss, we need to look at ministering to the person facing death. Whether the person is at home, in the hospital, or in hospice care, the pastor's approach at each visit is the same: encourage the person to talk; listen attentively; deal with fears and unresolved issues; and seek to make Christ real in the valley of the shadow. It may take time for the person to open up, and this must not be forced. Are there conflicts that must be settled? Has the patient thought about the funeral service?

Bring Bible truth into the conversation and don't hesitate to discuss death and the hereafter. If the person's death is a slow trajectory, you may have time to do a Bible study on death and heaven. If death is imminent, major on the great assurance passages, such as John 14:1–6; Romans 8:28–39; 2 Corinthians 5:1–8; and Psalm 23. Give the patient opportunity to affirm his or her faith in Christ; this will allow you to speak with confidence to the family and to the friends at the funeral. If there is no such affirmation of faith, with gentle urgency explain the love of Christ and the gospel and ask the patient to receive Christ. If there is resistance, don't threaten or frighten the person, but do urge him or her to make this all-important commitment to Christ.

Keep in mind that dying can be hard work, in spite of all the medication and fine equipment science has provided. Cancer can cause excruciating pain. Congestive heart failure makes it increasingly difficult to breathe. While medications ease the pain, they may also compromise the patient's alertness and awareness. While patients are conscious, we must seek to prepare them for the battle ahead and reassure them of God's presence (Psalm 23:4).

THE DYING PATIENT AT HOME

In an ideal world, we would die at home, in our own bed, surrounded by the people we love the most; but this isn't an ideal world. Most family members are more than willing to honor the requests of a dying loved one, but they may not want the death to occur in their home. In our opinion, hospice has a marvelous ministry for the terminal patient in the home, but they have time limitations for residential patients in their hospice facilities. Before a family turns the home into a hospital, they must honestly answer a number of practical questions.

- Where will the patient be located? Is this convenient to bathing facilities?

- What special equipment will we need, such as oxygen, hospital bed, wheelchair, inhaler, portable toilet, etc.?
- Will we have to remodel for handicap-accessible entries, shower, and the like?
- Can we prepare and serve special diets?
- How will pain management be handled? Will we need a licensed person to administer some medications?
- Are we as a family prepared to accept interruptions day and night and witness the suffering and eventually the death of the loved one?
- If a residential caregiver is required, do we have the space?

Then there's a very personal question: what is our motive for wanting to care for the person at home? Many elderly people don't want to go to a care facility and may put the family on a painful guilt trip as they plead to be left at home; but the care facility might provide better care and be just what they need. If the demands of home care are something the family isn't equipped to meet (and many aren't), the patient will be better off in a licensed care facility. The best reason for home care is, "We love her, and we want to do this, no matter what the demands or the sacrifices."

A third consideration is, What is the family's attitude toward death? If the family has a wholesome Christian view of death and doesn't try to deny it, then the patient will be in an atmosphere of faith and hope; but if anybody in the household is negative or even fearful, their discomfort will probably affect the patient. (Perhaps the patient will do them good!) We have seen situations where the dying person accepted the fact of death and wanted to talk about it, but the family would not discuss death at all. But there have also been times when the patient refused to face the reality of death, and this hindered the family's efforts to talk openly and prepare adequately. As caregivers, we can't force people to confront their last enemy. We can only open the communications door and hope that the people involved will step through it.

The family needs spiritual care as much as the patient, and we must seek to understand the dynamics of the home. Is the situation tense or relaxed? Are family members united in their faith and love? How are the younger members responding? Are the right people making the right decisions? Do the same problems or issues keep coming up in conversations? Are the adult members of the family openly dealing with the prospect of death and helping the patient to make plans? Do they seek your counsel and value it? Sometimes we must talk with family members privately and individually to discover these things.

Most church members expect the pastor to read Scripture and pray when visiting the home. Some families like to pray the Lord's Prayer together and even sing a verse of a hymn. Keep home ministry brief, and don't let it become routine or shallow. If you are present when the patient dies, a brief prayer and the quoting of relevant Scriptures will help prepare the way for the decisions and actions that must follow. (See chapter 5.) Don't rush the family. They may want to wait quietly by the body before getting caught up in the demands of the funeral plans.

THE DYING PATIENT IN THE HOSPITAL

The lady on the phone was speaking at warp speed.

"Pastor, the ambulance took her to the hospital and they don't think she was breathing and I just found out about it myself and I don't know what to think but I knew Bob would want me to call you—so what should I do?"

"First, take a deep breath. This is Janet, isn't it?"

"Yes. Sorry. I'm so shook I'm not thinking clearly."

"It's OK, Janet. Now, who was taken in the ambulance?"

"Catherine, my sister-in-law—Bob's sister."

"Tell me what happened."

"Well, she was working in her sewing room, and Bob called her about something but she didn't respond. He found her slumped on the worktable with the needlework still in her hand. He called 911 and they got there in just a couple of minutes, but I guess she wasn't breathing."

"Janet, where are Bob and Catherine's family now?"

"They've all gone to the hospital. Her husband rode in the ambulance. The kids have gone on their own. So did Bob's parents. I'm going as soon as I hang up."

"Janet, are you sure you're fit to drive? You still sound out of breath."

"I'm better now, really. You've helped me calm down."

"OK. I'll meet you at the hospital, but let's pray first." He offered a brief prayer, hung up, quickly told the church secretary the facts, and then headed for his car.

When calls come that you are needed immediately at the hospital, respond calmly and try to lower the caller's anxiety. Without being stoical, caregivers must control their own emotions so they can think clearly, trust the Lord, and bring some calm in the midst of storm. Many laypeople are uncomfortable in a hospital environment, and the combination of bad news and an intensive-care waiting room is enough to make people nervous. Your own controlled comfort level can help others feel more at ease. It's here that we trust the Spirit of God, the Comforter, to assist us.

Family members will want to get immediate information about the patient, but as we saw in chapter 4, federal HIPAA guidelines control who can say what to whom. In a crisis hour, this can be exasperating, but the doctors in charge will talk to the nearest of kin as soon as they know something definite. If you are present when the doctor talks to the family or the patient, perhaps you can ask a question or two, but for the most part, maintain your support ministry, silently pray, and wait. Staying with family members in the nearest waiting room will encourage them and keep all of you from getting in the way of the busy medical staff.

AT HOSPICE

The words *host, hospital,* and *hospice* come from the same Latin root meaning "to receive a guest, to give care to a stranger." During the Middle Ages, churches often provided "guesthouses" where travelers, the sick, paupers, orphans, and other needy people could find help. The hospice movement for the dying was begun in 1879 in Dublin by the Irish Sisters of Charity as a ministry to terminal cancer patients. It provided help in pain management, quiet time with loved ones, and spiritual strength for dealing with death. The ministry was adopted in London, England, in 1905, and after World War II it expanded rapidly and moved to the United States. At-home hospice care is available almost everywhere today, and many hospitals have inpatient hospice facilities.

Medical personnel in hospitals are certainly concerned about the emotional problems of patients, but their major task is to seek to control and cure disease and injury and to relieve pain, and it would be considered unethical for them to deal with spiritual matters. But hospice focuses primarily on the spiritual needs of the patient, the fears and concerns that center on death and dying. The spiritual is uppermost. The full-time staff and volunteers in hospice are well trained, compassionate, and professional in every way. If a patient wants to die at home, hospice makes that possible and relieves the family of duties they might not be able to handle. This gives the family time to spend with the dying loved one. Hospice also provides "respite care" so that the family caregivers can have some time off and the patient can have a change of venue for a short time. Usually a patient's life expectancy must be six months or less for hospice to provide care, but they are flexible.

EVEN IF THE PATIENT DOESN'T SEEM CONSCIOUS,
GO RIGHT AHEAD AND QUIETLY
READ THE SCRIPTURES AND PRAY.

Pastoral visits at hospice are relatively easy since the emphasis at hospice is on the spiritual. You find much less "activity" there, uninterrupted conversations are the norm, and the atmosphere is conducive to faith, hope, and love. Some patients actually improve while at hospice. Even if the patient doesn't seem conscious, go right ahead and quietly read the Scriptures and pray, because hearing is often the sense that functions to the very end. When death comes, the hospice workers will call the funeral director and help to guide the family through the decisions they must make.

NOTIFYING A FAMILY OF A DEATH

Following a fatal automobile accident, the police chaplain or fire/rescue unit chaplain usually notifies the family of the death. The death of service personnel is communicated by an official military visit to the home of the deceased. However, there are times when a pastor is asked to break the sad news. If you know the family socially, or if they are part of your congregation, then you will know what to say and do. But if the people are strangers to you, here are some guidelines to follow.

If you are notified by phone, get the caller's name, address, title, and phone number, as well as the name and phone number of someone who can officially confirm that the person has died. Be sure to have all the official information you need for the home visit: name, age, address, details of the death, where the body is, name of the ambulance company or number of the rescue unit, and names and phone numbers of those who can answer questions (witnesses, doctors, first responders).

We must go to the home in person and convey the sad news. If we phone, they may think it's a practical joke, or the call may come at a time when the family member is alone. If you know people in your congregation who know them and can be alerted, ask them to go along. Neighbors can also be very helpful at a time like this.

When the door opens, immediately identify yourself (your business card should be sufficient) and ask if you may come in to see the family. Be kind but get to the point: "I'm very sorry to tell you that your husband and father died of a heart attack while driving home from work. Witnesses saw the car veer off the road and hit a tree and stop. They called an ambulance, but the rescue workers were unable to revive him. He was taken to General Hospital, where further efforts also failed. That's where he is now."

If there are small children in the home, you may want to talk to the spouse and any other adults alone, and then they can share the news with the younger ones. Stay long enough to answer questions and help them with whatever decisions they have to make. *Make it very clear that you are not an ambulance chaser who is looking for a funeral to conduct.* If you learn who their pastor is, you can phone him. If the family desires, you can contact friends or neighbors to be with them. If there are little children in the home, a babysitter may be needed. Perhaps other family members in town can come to help.

The scene will have a surreal quality about it, and you may be asked if you are joking or what authority you have to be there. In some situations, they may become very angry and take out their anger on the messenger. "This too will pass," so the "soft answer" is your best response. You can offer to take some of the family to the hospital (or wherever the body is), while the others get their act together; and they may need your help in going through the funeral preparation. Their own pastor should do this for them, but answer their questions and stay on hand until he arrives on the scene.

Watch the obituary column for information and extend your sympathy by means of a personal visit, a phone call, or a card. If this is an unchurched family, this may be an opportunity to make new friends for the Lord and His church.

TRAGIC DEATH IN THE FAMILY

Except for Christian terminal patients who are yearning for heaven, any death is tragic, but some deaths are more tragic than others and bring with them special problems.

MURDER

If you have a passion for exact numbers, then here's one for you: according to the FBI, 14,054 persons were murdered in the United States in 2002. That's only a number—until one of those victims is somebody you know, especially if it's someone in your own family. Consider the problems involved. First, the family has no time to prepare for the news, so they will need a support team as soon as possible, people to answer the phone, run errands, notify other family members and friends, and especially pray. Then, the police must conduct a site search at the scene of the crime, and this takes time. They also must interrogate family members and friends, so a trip to headquarters may be in order. Family members may have to go to the scene of the crime and perhaps to the morgue. We've seen all these things acted out on television, but this time, it's real.

Grief will focus not only on the death itself but also on the manner of the death—murder, perhaps very brutal and very ugly. The murderer robbed the victim of life and a family of a loved one, and the mourners cry out for immediate justice. "It's not fair" is an honest statement, but we live in a dangerous world, and anything can happen. Anger and grief mingle, people feel helpless, and only God's grace can give peace. The circumstances raise questions. Was this a random murder? Is somebody after the whole family? Why us? Why didn't God prevent this? Are we all being punished? If so, for what? We wish there were satisfying answers to all these questions, but sometimes all we can do is speculate. People live on promises and not on explanations, so focus on God's Word.

Since most murders draw in the press, the family may have to appoint someone to be their spokesperson. Murders also attract the curious, so the family must take steps to protect their privacy. For thoughts about the funeral of a murder victim, see chapter 9.

SUDDEN DEATH

No, not the kind that breaks a tie in a basketball or hockey game, but the kind that breaks into a family unexpectedly and takes away a loved one. Life is fragile. Cars crash, electric wires strike pedestrians, a driver backing up doesn't see a child on the driveway, a heart stops beating, a tornado touches down—and life is over for people who hadn't expected to die that day. The family has no warning, so once again a support system is needed as soon as possible. Go to the family where they are, mobilize the congregation for support, and help the family as they make decisions. Family members are shocked, and the shock may last a long time. We dare not protect them from the reality of their loss and pain, but we can point them to God's faithful promises. Romans 8:28 says that God is working all things together for good *here and now*—not just at some future time—and we can trust Him.

One typical problem is anger. "Why did she do this *now*?" But she didn't "do this"—it happened, and she didn't have an opportunity to vote on the matter. Death usually creates family problems, sudden death even more. Perhaps the victim didn't have a will, or maybe he or she didn't leave any instructions for the funeral and burial. For many of the families whose loved ones died in the Twin Towers attack (9/11) or the bombing of the Murrah Federal Building in Oklahoma City on April 19, 1995, the sudden loss of the loved one also included the loss of the remains. There was no face to see, no hand to touch, and today there is no grave to visit. Yes, there were memorial services, but the absence of the body means the services may not have left memories that might help the mourners heal. As caregivers, we can assist the families in remembering by turning over the pages of the photo albums, looking at family videos, and rehearsing the things about the deceased that mean the most to those they loved.

'IN THE LINE OF DUTY'

September 11, 2001, brought us face-to-face with the dangers faced by our brave police officers, firefighters, and others who serve and protect the community. And, at this writing, American troops are engaged in Iraq, and we hear each week about military personnel (and civilians) being killed by bullets or suicide bombers. Sometimes "friendly fire" kills a person, or it may be the crash of a helicopter.

Those who serve in enforcing the law, fighting fires, or fighting wars know that their chosen work is dangerous, but they face the risks and serve faithfully. Their families know all about the occupational hazards and are proud of what they are doing and pray for them. When tragedy comes, the family will be informed by the chaplain or other authorized official, and the family will in turn notify the pastor.

As soon as you get word that there has been a death "in the line of duty," go to the family and stay with the family as long as necessary. In the case of death in the military, it will take time for the remains to be sent home, so stay close to the family without being a nuisance. You may want to accompany them to the airport when the body arrives. Local military people will enlighten you about your part in a military funeral. (For suggestions about military funerals, see chapter 8.) You may want to give some special recognition in the worship service on the Sunday following the interment.

THE DEATH OF A CHILD

Approximately 228,000 children and young adults under forty die in the United States each year, not including stillbirths and miscarriages. About 19 percent of the adult population has experienced the death of a child and 22 percent the death of a sibling. A child's death is an event that says, "There's something out of order in this world," for parents don't expect to outlive their children. They not only grieve the loss of the child but also the loss of the future, for the future rests with the children. Grieving parents will not see their hopes and dreams materialize for that child.

Life is always precarious, but risks are higher at certain times of life, and birth and early childhood are high-risk times. Miscarriage and stillbirth are the most common neonatal concerns, and physical complications, illness, and Sudden Infant Death Syndrome (SIDS) are major postpartum concerns. According to the SIDS Family Web site, SIDS is the most common cause of death during the first year of a child's life. Death is no respecter of children, for about 3,000 infants die of SIDS each year. After bonding with the child for nine months, the mother feels the loss very deeply. But children and youths also die in accidents and from diseases and abuse. They are murdered and, according to Marion Duckworth, each year almost 5,000 youths ages 15–24 commit suicide (*Why Teens are Killing Themselves*, p. 14).

While experiencing grief, parents sometimes also experience guilt. Parents expect to "fix" their children's problems and protect them from danger, and the "what-ifs" can be grief-blockers that hinder normal healing. Couples need to be reminded that men and women grieve differently, husbands preferring to grieve alone and wives wanting to be held as they openly allow their feelings to pour out. The more frankly they both can discuss their hurts and needs, the healthier the grief and the marriage will be. One indicator of what kind of progress is being made is the situation in the child's room. Has the room remained unchanged—a shrine—or has it been converted into usable space without removing reminders of the child?

For years it was believed that parents who have had a child die are at very high risk for divorcing, but a survey commissioned by Compassionate Friends, Inc., shows that only 12 percent have had that experience (*When a Child Dies: A Survey of Bereaved Parents*, pp. 5–6). It's very unwise for the spiritual caregiver to bring up the matter of divorce. If you see some signs of alienation and withdrawal developing between the husband and wife, or perhaps persistent bickering, accusation, and blame, then you must intervene and suggest they get professional help.

We suggest holding a memorial service for a miscarried child. Some couples have already named the child, so they will take the death very personally. A service allows them to publicly acknowledge the death, and it also permits family and friends to share love and encouragement.

What about the siblings of a child who dies? Their grief is just as real as that of the adults in the family, so they should not be ignored as the parents make plans. Nobody can really explain the death of a child, but we can listen to the other children's questions and seek to allay their fears. If they don't attend the funeral, will they wonder what's going on and why they were left out? "What else aren't they telling me?" they might ask themselves. "Am I also in danger of dying?" Children can write a letter to the deceased sibling, or draw a picture, and thereby show their grief in a concrete way. Some families have drawn a picture together. As the children get older, they will ask questions and better understand the answers we try to give. *Parents must always answer with the truth, and children must never be told something about a death that must be "untold" later on.* There are times when the parents must grieve, but they must also care for the family. The best way to honor the dead is to take care of the living.

CHILDREN MUST NEVER BE TOLD SOMETHING ABOUT A DEATH THAT MUST BE 'UNTOLD' LATER ON.

We must not ignore the grandparents in these times of sorrow, for they find themselves having to be comforters to their own children and grandchildren. Grandparents see both the future and the past in their grandchildren ("She was just like you at that age"), and this gives them a double burden to bear. In many families, there are strong bonds between the older and younger generations, and this must not be minimized. The grandfather who took little Matthew out to breakfast every Saturday morning will miss him keenly next week and on the Saturdays to follow.

A DEATH COMPLICATED BY AIDS

Even though it seems that in recent years we've been hearing less about AIDS in the United States and more about AIDS in Africa, the illness has not gone away, and the wise caregiver will be prepared to offer compassionate ministry to its victims. Acquired Immune Deficiency Syndrome is caused by the human immunodeficiency virus (HIV), which is transmitted by an exchange of bodily fluids (blood, semen). The virus is not transmitted by a handshake or a hug. At this writing, there is no known cure, although improved medication and treatment have helped to give length and quality of life to many AIDS patients. AIDS patients usually die from disease complications caused by the inadequacy of the immune system, such as pneumonia. In 2003, about 950,000 people in the United States tested HIV-positive.

And the church is integrally involved in their care. According to the AIDS National Interfaith Network, there are over three thousand ministries in eleven national AIDS networks working with AIDS patients every day. More than half of all community-based AIDS organizations are operated by the religious community. It's unfortunate that many AIDS patients are abandoned by their families for one reason or another, but there are people ready to step in and help in the name of God. Missionaries in hospitals around the world are caring for AIDS patients and sharing Christ's love.

Regardless of how the patient acquired the virus, he or she is a person created in the image of God and loved by God, a person for whom Jesus died, and it's up to God's people to demonstrate God's love. The care we give must be shaped by a willingness to accept the patients even if we disagree with their values or lifestyles. This means listening to the feelings behind their words and allowing them to be angry, to ask tough questions, and even to declare war on God. They can't change the past—but they can make strategic decisions today that will affect their future. Affirm the patient as a person, not a hopeless sinner. Build trust, offer hope, and point to Jesus Christ and His abundant grace.

AIDS may greatly—and adversely—affect the dynamics of the family. The person with AIDS may feel bitter and abandoned; his family members may be angry or ashamed. A faithful wife may be struggling with her HIV-positive husband who just came out of the closet. The pastor can help family members, if not wholly understand, at least listen to one another.

If the patient brings up the matter of the funeral, listen carefully, make suggestions where necessary, and take notes. Chat with members of the family about what you have learned, and let them help make decisions. Nobody can accurately predict how long any patient will live, but AIDS patients know that they don't dare indulge in futile speculations. Once the patient accepts the facts of life and death, it's easier for everybody—the patient, family and friends, the medical team, and the caregivers. The Christian caregiver seeks to lead the patient to faith in Christ, for He alone can give the courage and peace needed.

SUICIDE

The National Center for Health Statistics reported 31,655 suicides in

2002, and about 30,000 is the average for any year. That's one every twenty minutes. But we must also consider the 130,000 who are hospitalized for attempting suicide and the 115,000 who are treated and released in various emergency facilities. *Suicide is the third leading cause of death for young people from ages 10 to 24.* The suicide rate for people 65 and older is increasing. Experts in this field tell us that the figures for suicides are actually greater than reported because many "accidents" are really suicides, but the "accident" cannot be confirmed as a suicide and the authorities want to spare the family more grief.

When a suicide occurs, the grieving family finds itself being attacked by some very powerful forces. They are bewildered over why the loved one committed suicide, and angry at what seems to be a very selfish and foolish act. They feel guilty ("Where did we fail?"), helpless ("Why didn't we understand the signals?"), and concerned over what people will think and say. The surviving family members feel stigmatized and ashamed, and yet the matter must be faced courageously and dealt with honestly.

Why do people kill themselves? We may never know for sure. Why do professed Christians take their own lives? We know that Satan is a murderer and a liar (John 8:44) and would drive all of us to hopeless despair if we gave him a foothold. Sometimes people take their lives just to punish others, and they will do it on a birthday or at Christmas so the event will be remembered annually. If most people who contemplate suicide would sit down and calmly discuss their problems with a competent counselor or even a loving friend, they would see that they were making a big mistake in planning to destroy themselves.

For some people, when the problems of life so far outweigh the pleasures, they feel trapped and want to end it all. There are no conclusive studies, but it seems that seemingly insoluble financial difficulties, worsening relational problems, and terminal illnesses rank high as "reasons" for suicide. To what extent mental conditions are involved, nobody can say for sure. People slowly dying of a lingering illness grow weary of medication, treatments, and even of people, and they long for the privilege of a quiet exit.

There was a time when some Christian communions would not allow the body of a suicide victim to be buried in "consecrated ground," but that attitude has changed. The belief that a person who commits suicide automatically goes to hell is also no longer used as a deterrent. Judas went to hell, not because he committed suicide, but because he did not believe in Jesus Christ and was a counterfeit Christian (Matthew 27:5; Acts 1:25; John 6:66–71). The Bible teaches that life is a precious gift from God, and that we are forbidden to kill. It also affirms that nothing can separate us from the love of God (Romans 8:31–39). However, nobody has the privilege of going into God's presence without an invitation. If we do, the first thing the Father will say to us is, "You did a very foolish thing."

Relatives of a murder victim or a suicide usually experience an extended grieving period, and official investigations and court proceedings, some of which drag on for years after the fact, don't make it easier. Let's keep in touch with the family and allow the Lord to use us to encourage faith, hope, and love through the Word and prayer. For us to act like legal experts or professional police investigators is to add to their problems. We represent the King of Glory and must ask God to help us represent Him well. One day the painful problems of life will be untangled and we shall know even as we are known. Until then, goodness and mercy are following us, and the Father's house is not too far down the road.

AFTER THE FUNERAL

This may be when the real pastoral care begins. Grieving persons usually need pastoral care and encouragement for weeks after they have laid a loved one to rest. When death occurs, neighbors, friends, and the church family immediately step in with support and various forms of practical assistance. But after a few days, the relatives go home and the friends tend to drift back to their normal routine.

But bereaved people have no routine, because nothing seems normal anymore. After the flurry of death-related activities—sending out thank-you notes, paying bills, contacting insurance companies and other organizations, finalizing details at the cemetery, and changing everything from bank accounts to magazine subscriptions—the mourner is weary, yet with "nothing to do." Of course, there *are* things to do, because life goes on, but something has happened to her motivation and energy. The widow or widower is now a "single," and this changes their relationship to many other people. At this point, the spiritual caregiver must step in and help to build some bridges both to the past and the future.

Nobody has a predictable journey through grief, so we must be patient and discerning. It's better to call frequently and keep the visits brief than to visit occasionally and stay too long. Enlist others in the church to help in this ministry, and take them with you so they see how to do it. The sooner mourners return to worship services and their accustomed activities, the faster they will recover, but they must not be forced to put on a front just to please their friends. That can only make matters worse.

In any case, whatever their journey, they will need you—the provider of Christian care—to help them through it.

Death and the Final Good-Bye

The average family is familiar with paying for the professional services of physicians, plumbers, and auto mechanics, but sitting in the office of a funeral director is usually a new and challenging experience for them. During a time of sorrow, they are asked to make wise decisions about difficult matters. How much to pay? What sort of service to have?

As we have seen, Jessica Mitford's *The American Way of Death* not only documented certain abuses she saw in the funeral industry, but it also criticized the funeral itself. Even today, for whatever reasons, many people wonder why we continue to conduct funerals when they seem so unnecessary. A cynic might define a funeral as an obsolete but expensive tradition that enriches the funeral director, upsets the preacher's busy schedule, snarls the traffic, entertains the spectators, and adds to the grief of the mourners, especially when they receive the bill. But that certainly isn't the Christian point of view.

According to Mitford, the average undertaker's bill for casket and services is about $4,700. When you add other expenses—burial vault, cemetery charges, clothing, flowers, services of musicians, and so on—

the price may be as high as $7,800.[1] In spite of shocking stories about high-pressure salesmanship at a time when sorrowing people are vulnerable, most staff people in a funeral home are thoughtful and patient and want the family to select merchandise and services that they feel are appropriate and affordable.

We also need to remember that more is involved in professional funeral preparation than most people realize. From the first service call to pick up the body to the cleaning up of the chapel and parking lot after the service, the funeral director could easily spend more than thirty hours per funeral. He must also add more time for the preparation of the body if it was not in good shape, and this could include plastic surgery. The funeral director is the family's representative at the cemetery and, if the body is to be cremated, at the crematorium.

But if the cost of a funeral seems high, keep in mind that, like a wedding or a retirement dinner, what we spend is a statement of the value of the life being celebrated. Yes, spending can be overdone, and sometimes hidden guilt encourages unnecessary extravagance. But why should people be robbed of the privilege of saying good-bye in a way that satisfies them?

'SO THAT HE MIGHT HAVE THE SUPREMACY'

Yet as we say good-bye, we must do so in such a way that *God is glorified*—which, Scripture tells us, should underlie everything we do as believers (1 Corinthians 10:31). Not all believers will be martyrs like Peter (John 21:18–19) and Paul (Philippians 1:20–21), but we should still glorify God in everything related to life and death. Our last will and testimony shared at the funeral is as important as our last will and testament read in the lawyer's office, and both should reflect God's will. The focus of the service must be on God and His glory as revealed in the gospel of Jesus Christ, "so that in everything he might have the supremacy" (Colossians 1:18). No matter what problems people face, the one answer the Father has provided for us is His Son, Jesus Christ. He is what we need, and He is all we need, and we want to honor Him.

This means that the funeral is, essentially, a worship service. The center of attention is not a dead body but the living God. The family may want the casket open for a short time before the service so that friends can view the body, but it should be closed before the service begins and not opened publicly again. That the service is one of worship also means that the congregation should be participants and not just spectators. Depending on the desires of the family, you may want to include a brief congregational Scripture reading and perhaps even a hymn of praise. This is no problem when the service is held in a church where pew Bibles and hymnals are available. At a funeral home chapel service, if you want congregational participation, you will have to prepare worship folders to be handed out to the guests. Of course, you must also consider the size of the group.

AT A FUNERAL, THE CENTER OF ATTENTION
IS NOT A DEAD BODY BUT THE LIVING GOD.

A second purpose for the funeral is to *dignify human life created by God.* We are made in the image of God, and the body of the believer is the temple of God, sealed by the Holy Spirit (Ephesians 1:13–14; 4:30). People who complain because "funerals are body centered" must remember that life itself is "body centered," because most of what we know about each other relates to the body. Husbands and wives are one flesh, and the death of a spouse is like the amputation of a limb. Children are our own flesh and blood, and no matter how old they are when they die, parents feel the pain. The funeral service reminds us that dead people are not dead animals to be disposed of like roadkill. Human beings are the crowning work of God's creation, and the funeral service announces this.

The funeral is not just the recognition of a death and a step toward accepting it, but it's also the celebration of a life. Long and elaborate eulogies are no longer a part of the average funeral, unless the deceased is famous and the media people are on hand. However, for a family member—or several of them—to give words of personal appreciation (written out and read) adds to the living witness of the deceased. The celebration of a life is an encouragement to the living, as well as a commemoration of the dead.

It's unfortunate that novelty has crept into some funeral services, the kind of novelty that trivializes death and human dignity. We have in our file a newspaper clipping with a photo of a dead man sitting in a casket that was made to look like an automobile—steering wheel, lights, wheels, and all. The family "wanted him to go out in style," the photo caption affirms. You can also buy caskets made of a specially coated wood on which people may write messages to be taken to the grave. The argument is that different people need different ways to cope with their sorrow, and whatever helps is acceptable. Anyway, say the manufacturers, writing on a casket isn't much different from signing a cast for somebody who has a broken arm or leg. Perhaps, but we feel that these novelties trivialize human life, because they trivialize death and the celebration of life.

This leads to a third purpose for the funeral: *to remind people that life is precious and brief, a gift from God not to be wasted.* Most people don't think about it, but they spend a great deal of time, energy, and money just trying to stay alive, and yet many of them do their best to deny that death even exists—as we saw in chapter 1. The denial of death seems to be an important part of American culture. It's a "youth culture" supported by industries that make people miserable if they don't feel young, look young, and act young. We have opportunity at a funeral service or memorial service to remind the living that life is a privilege that must not be wasted or merely spent. It must be invested in that which really counts. With the celebration of life also comes the evaluation of life. "Teach us to number our days aright, that we may gain a heart of wisdom" (Psalm 90:12).

This means, of course, that we preach the Word and declare the gospel. No, the funeral service is not a high-powered evangelistic meeting during which we take advantage of people and "let 'em have it," like shooting fish in a barrel. If the total service is planned carefully and presented in the Spirit's power, the gospel message will be clear.

Our fourth purpose is *to give comfort to hurting people.* This is a ministry of the church as a whole and not the pastor only, and congregations need to be reminded that the members of the Christian family must support and encourage one another in the crisis experiences of life. "Rejoice with those who rejoice; mourn with those who mourn" is a command from God (Romans 12:15). The English word *comfort* comes from two Latin words that together mean "with strength." We comfort others when God uses us to enable them to have strength to accept His will and carry on in spite of loss and pain. Shallow sympathy and empty sentimental words only make matters worse, because they reveal our lack of understanding of how others really feel in their sorrows.

The Holy Spirit, the divine Comforter, gives us the comfort we need. We realize that our Father knows our situation and cares for us and that our Savior is interceding for us and shares our grief. No matter how much we hurt, we know that Jesus suffered far more and did it for our sake. If we accept God's will by faith, the Holy Spirit imparts the grace we need and enables us to use our suffering for our good, the good of others, and the glory of God. We are "more than conquerors" (Romans 8:37), which, among other things, means that we *enlist* our suffering and don't just *endure* it.

Job named his so-called friends "miserable comforters" with "long-winded speeches" (Job 16:1–3), because they neither understood his heart nor spoke the truth in love. They had mastered all the traditional and approved answers to the trials of life, but they didn't know how to convey comfort from the Lord. True comforters don't necessarily do a lot of talking. They know how to listen, and sometimes they do more good with their silences than with their words. More than once grieving members of the church family have thanked us for "just being there" when they first went to the funeral home to view the body. All we did was stand silently, praying for the family and not saying too much. The healing silence of a loving heart shares much comfort. There is always time later to share God's Word and talk over personal problems.

There is an important fifth purpose that the critics of funerals sometimes overlook: *the funeral is an important step toward helping the mourners accept the reality and finality of the death and the responsibility of dealing with their grief in a mature way.* The popular television psychologist Dr. Joyce Brothers put it this way:

When a loved one dies, grief spins a complicated web of emotion, which cannot be brushed aside, but which must be owned up to, endured, and gradually untangled skein by skein. If these feelings are denied in their proper season, they will return to haunt the mourner later on.[2]

Writing about the people who have yet to find their loved ones after the World Trade Center tragedy on September 11, 2001, Nicholas Wade points out that when there is no body to see and touch, mourners find it difficult to accept the death and handle their emotions successfully. "We're biodegradable but some mysterious programming deep in our minds insists on a respectful decomposition." Society treats death as a medical event, says Wade, "but in the dark recesses of our minds it is more."[3] Grief counselors tell us that people who try to live with unresolved grief often develop problems that can't be solved by tranquilizers and long vacations. There must be closure in both the heart and the mind, and a proper funeral service can help to provide it.

THE TRADITIONAL CHRISTIAN FUNERAL

Surveys indicate that American funerals are pretty standard, except for ethnic and religious groups that have their own special traditions. A funeral must not be generic, a "one-size-fits-all" presentation. It must be personal with the name of the deceased being mentioned. People come from the dust and go back to the dust, but in between, they deserve some kind of identification. Dust is anonymous, but people have names.

The minister should find out from the family just what kind of service they have in mind. The deceased may even have left some written directions, and we should comply as much as possible. We recall a woman

DUST IS ANONYMOUS, BUT PEOPLE HAVE NAMES.

who left a request in writing that a tenor sing the old song "The Indian Love Call" at her memorial service. (She had donated her body to a medical school.) We found a tenor, and he sang the song beautifully. His solo was perfect preparation for a message from John 11:28, "The Master is come, and calleth for thee" (KJV). The service may have opened on Broadway, but it ended at Calvary and the empty tomb, and nobody seemed to be offended because the gospel was preached. However, sometimes people make requests that are so far-out we don't dare accept them but must gently yet firmly suggest alternatives.

The order of service usually includes:

An opening statement of affirmation to call the congregation to order
A brief prayer of invocation
Scripture reading or congregational Scripture reading
Music (optional)
Eulogy (optional)
Message
Congregational hymn (optional)
Benediction

There are many possible combinations. If the deceased has a grandson who is a gifted pianist, he can play a hymn in Grandma's honor. Family participation can help bring love and healing, but please don't turn the service into an amateur hour. Another family member could read the eulogy, and keep in mind that in these cases, family humor is permitted. We will never forget a college-age grandson saying, "And Grandpa even went out and bought a pair of jeans!" The chuckle that rippled across the congregation was just what we needed at that point in the service.

It's a basic rule that if anybody is asked to say something at a funeral, what they say must be first written out. Most people aren't experienced public speakers, and they have a tendency to ramble if asked to speak extemporaneously; so sticking to a text is important. Children may be "cute" in what they say and do, but a funeral isn't the place to demonstrate cuteness and cleverness.

BEFORE THE MESSAGE

We suggest you open the service by quoting or reading 1 John 3:1–2 and 1 Peter 1:3–5. Then say, "Because of these great certainties, we meet today to honor the life and grieve the death of [name the deceased]. We sorrow, but not as those who have no hope." Here quote or read 1 Thessalonians 4:13–18, then pray briefly as you invoke the help of the Lord.

If the family requests a favorite Scripture reading, it can follow the invocation. Perhaps they want a member of the family to do it, so be sure the person is prepared. The public reading of the Word of God is not a ministry for amateurs. Another option is a congregational responsive reading, but you will have to provide the text, unless you meet in a church where hymnals are available.

The matter of music at a funeral is purely personal. If the deceased requested a hymn or that somebody sing a solo, then we should try to comply. We note that more and more "secular songs" are being used at so-called Christian funerals, and this is a bit disturbing. A friend of ours who ministers in music at funerals was asked to sing the Frank Sinatra theme song "I Did It My Way," and another soloist we know was told the family wanted him to sing the deceased's favorite, "Home on the Range." We can't conceive of dedicated believers making these choices, but these things are happening, and we must be prepared to deal with them and somehow relate to them in the message.

A eulogy (Greek *eulogia* = good words) is more than an obituary, because it presents the deceased in a living way that expands the bare facts in the obituary. It should be read by a member of the family or a close friend, it should not be too long, and it should tell the truth but not exaggerate or embarrass. The Latin proverb still applies: *De mortuis nil nisi bene*—"Say nothing but good of the dead." "Consideration for the dead, who no longer need it, is dearer to us than the truth," warned Freud, so we must be careful to be honest. Perhaps you heard about the brother who was eulogizing the deceased church member and waxing eloquent. The widow whispered to one of her children, "Go up and see if that's really your daddy in that casket."

SHARING THE TRUTH IN LOVE

Every message that we preach must be biblical, organized, practical, and easy to follow; but a funeral message needs special crafting. It must not be a detailed exposition of a text, nor should it be presented in a manner that "sounds like a sermon." We've always felt that the minister should use a calm, conversational style at a funeral, as though chatting with the people in their living room. At one funeral, we heard a learned exposition of 1 Corinthians 15 (including Greek exegesis), and everything the pastor said was biblical, but the message didn't do us much good. It was like reading the recipe instead of eating the meal. Had he chosen one central vivid truth from that great chapter—and there are many of them—and presented it with imagination, he would have reached our hearts and brought comfort. Few mourners bring Bibles to funerals, so they're unable to follow a verse-by-verse exposition that would be welcomed in a Sunday school class or a morning worship service. Leave the Hebrew and Greek and theological vocabulary in the study and simply share the truth in love. We preach to express, not to impress.

Most preachers have a file of funeral outlines that are still useful, but we must seek to make each message individual, prepared for the occasion. As we have said, the key is to select one luminous biblical truth that relates to the deceased, focus on it, and make it personal and practical. A text that demands too much explanation will not do the job. As we mentioned earlier, sorrowing people need medicine for their hearts, not a theological doctor's prescription.

For example, one pastor used "Christ the Carpenter" (Mark 6:3) as his theme when conducting a service for a man whose vocation had been carpentry. He pointed out that Jesus was a builder, not a destroyer, and that today He is building a heavenly home for His people. He died the death of a carpenter, nailed to a cross of wood. If we trust Him, He will save us and build our lives according to God's perfect blueprint.

The message must center on God and His grace and not on people and their failures. It should look ahead and be radiant with hope. At the same time, it must be realistic and remind people that death is real, that grief is normal, that life is not easy, but that the Lord is adequate for every need.

When ministering to a family disturbed by bitterness that had long roots to it, the minister used the simple text, "But he gives us more grace" (James 4:6). He opened with "It's the gift of God's grace that saves us," and he lovingly explained the gospel of God's wonderful grace. Then he went on to show that God gives us more grace to help us in times of trial and difficulty. Without meddling in family affairs, he closed by showing how God's grace overrules even in our failures, and he used the story of Joseph to show how eventually God brings everything together. He closed with Annie Johnson Flint's beautiful poem "He Giveth More Grace." As he ministered to the family during the weeks that followed, he was able to see real progress in the righting of past wrongs and the healing of family hurts.

A funeral message is preached for the good of the living and not for the glory of the dead. That belongs in the eulogy. Although we may have a reasonable certainty of the spiritual condition of most of the people in our church family, it's unwise to preach anybody into either heaven or hell. God knows His own children (2 Timothy 2:19), and nobody knows what momentous transactions may have occurred in the final hours of a patient's life. Remember the thief on the cross.

Perhaps the word that best describes the ideal funeral message is *sensitivity*. We must be sensitive to the needs of the family and to the life and testimony (or lack of it) of the deceased. We must be sensitive to the message from the Word that the people need at that hour and apply it in a sensitive way. To dust off an old outline simply won't do. Take that old outline and ask God to breathe new life into it, and tailor it to the situation at hand. Surely we have learned something new since the last time we preached it! The funeral message must help turn the listeners' ears into eyes so they see the truth in a vivid way and receive it into their needy hearts. The loving shepherd who knows his sheep will have the right words to say.

PERHAPS THE WORD THAT BEST DESCRIBES
THE IDEAL FUNERAL MESSAGE IS *SENSITIVITY*.

We suggest that you begin what Andrew W. Blackwood called "a sermonic seed plot" where you plant seeds (texts and ideas for sermons) and give them time to grow. This can be a file folder or a notebook, but it receives your written records of ideas that later will develop into messages. When you least expect it, the Lord will teach you special truths relating to some of the "plants" you're nurturing, and you will have your message. It's impossible to schedule funerals weeks in advance, and we may have only a day or two to develop the message, and that's when the "seed plot" comes to our rescue.

Another suggestion is that you begin to think about texts for various people in the church. Some who are elderly, perhaps even in the hospital, deserve our best, and there's no reason we can't be pondering and praying about the funeral service. The messages for the "senior saints" who have been the pillars of the church ought to be very special. Of course, we never tell anybody that we're planning their funeral, because it would be misunderstood. (However, if we chat with them about the future, they may tell us their funeral is already planned!) What we're saying is that we must think ahead and plan ahead, capturing those fugitive ideas that come at unexpected times.

Please don't use a biblical text out of context, like a motto taken from a bumper sticker. It's true that "to depart and be with Christ . . . is far better" (Philippians 1:23), but the next verse says, "Nevertheless to remain in the flesh is more needful for you" (NKJV). Yes, the loved one is better off in heaven, but that doesn't mean that the mourners necessarily feel better off here on earth. When Jesus told His disciples He was returning to heaven, it was good news for Him but bad news for them, and He acknowledged it (John 14:27–31; 16:6). Unfortunately, the reality of heaven isn't as vivid to many believers today as it was to the saints in the difficult days of persecution, martyrdom, and overall high mortality rates. But heaven isn't just a *destination;* it's a *motivation* (Hebrews 11:10–14, 16, 26; 12:1–3), and the promise of eternal glory ought to make a difference in our lives on earth today. This includes dealing with our sorrows.

Another "motto verse" that shows up at funerals is Psalm 116:15, "Precious in the sight of the LORD is the death of his saints." If we ignore the context, we might give the impression that God enjoys seeing His people suffer and die and their loved ones sorrow; but of course, that isn't what it means at all. The writer of the psalm had been in great danger and had almost lost his life, but the Lord heard his prayers and rescued him. Why? Because in God's sight the death of a child of God is not an incident or an accident; it's an appointment that's very meaningful to Him. After all, the Father sent His Son to suffer and die that we might be saved and one day have a home in heaven. Our entrance into the Father's house is very costly, and that's why a believer's death is very precious in God's sight. If we quote this verse but don't explain it, we may send people home with wrong ideas about God and Christian death.

A funeral message need not be long, but it should be adequate. Remember, we're focusing on one luminous Bible truth and dealing with it in such as way that our listeners can see it and feel it. For example, Proverbs 4:18 declares that there is no "sunset" in the life of the Christian believer, in spite of what the songwriters say. God's children are walking a path that gets brighter and brighter and ends in the land of endless day.

"There will be no night there" (Revelation 21:25). This is a text people can see as well as hear. Ponder it.

Here are some other texts to consider and perhaps add to your "sermonic seed plot."

Exodus 16:7—God's glory in the morning

1 Samuel 1:27–28—a child given to the Lord

1 Samuel 20:3—only a step to death, and only a step of faith to life

2 Samuel 12:23—we shall meet in heaven infants who have died

Psalm 77:9—when people experience one tragedy after another

Proverbs 10:7—the growing influence of the memory of the godly

Proverbs 16:31—the coronation of the godly senior saint (see Isaiah 46:4)

Proverbs 31:30–31—the godly wife and mother

Ecclesiastes 3:11—faith gives things time to get beautiful

Isaiah 40:11—the Good Shepherd carries the little one close to His heart

Isaiah 43:1–5—God's presence and help in times of crisis

Isaiah 61:1–2 / Luke 4:16–19—the Great Physician heals broken hearts

Matthew 18:10—the Father's care of the children

Mark 10:13–16—Jesus welcomes the children

John 11:28—in the hour of sorrow, the Master calls for us

John 11:32—the questioning heart: "Lord, if . . ."

John 13:7—". . . later you will understand" (see 1 Corinthians 13:12)

Romans 8:38–39—even death can't separate us from God's love

Hebrews 9:27—death is an appointment, not an accident

Many of the images of death that we considered in chapters 2 and 3 make excellent texts for funeral messages, so consider them as well. In his book *The Funeral,* Andrew Blackwood devotes several pages to "sermonic seed plot" texts and categorizes them according to the characteristics of the deceased—child, youth, one who is aged, one who suffered greatly, and so on. It's unfortunate that this fine book is out of print.

'IT IS FINISHED'

The family may request that the congregation sing a hymn or perhaps listen to the ministry of a soloist, so introduce it by relating it to what you said in the message. "Life is a pilgrimage, but we know that for the believer, Jesus is our Shepherd and our journey ends in the Father's house. Ponder this truth as together we sing [or our soloist sings] the familiar 'Savior, Like a Shepherd Lead Us.'" Then follows the benediction, but please don't preach the message again as you pray. The priestly benediction of Numbers 6:24–26 is always suitable, as is Hebrews 13:20–21, but there are other verses that can easily be used as benedictions simply by turning them into prayers.

The conclusion of your benediction is the signal for the funeral director and pallbearers to escort the casket out of the room, and you may either walk at the head with the funeral director or walk with the family as they follow. However, some funeral chapels are designed so that the casket and flowers may be taken to the hearse and flower car from the front of the chapel through a large door. In that case, the pallbearers wait at the front and you walk out with the family and remain with them until the procession is ready to go to the cemetery.

If you ride to the cemetery in the hearse, be sure to keep the conversation on a high level. Unfortunately, some drivers think they should entertain the minister with funeral jokes or other questionable humor. Once they find out your stand, word will get around and this will stop. But, let's not be so pompous that we give the wrong impression of a Christian minister and the Christian faith.

The purpose of the brief committal service is simply to write "It is finished" over all that has been done. Unless mourners face the finality of death and accept it, they can't begin to heal and transition successfully back into life with its responsibilities. The minister walks before the casket with the funeral director, and the family and friends follow them as they all assemble at the open grave. The pastor stands at the head of the casket—the funeral director will identify it for you—and speaks so that everybody can hear. The committal service need not be long, but it should not be unnecessarily hurried. If the weather is inclement, the funeral director can tell the men not to take off their hats. One of the best ways to honor the dead is to be kind to the living.

At the graveside, we have usually emphasized the blessed hope that Christians have because of their salvation in Jesus Christ. The natural tendency at a cemetery is for people to look *down*, but we must encourage them to look *up* and *ahead* to the return of the Lord. The minister may say, "The word 'cemetery' means 'a sleeping place,' because this is where the body sleeps until the resurrection. The soul of the believer goes to be with the Lord, for to be absent from the body is to be present with the Lord. Our ancestors used to call the cemetery 'God's acre,' because here we plant the body like a humble seed, knowing that God will one day bring it forth in glory." This is a good place to read 1 Corinthians 15:42–44.

Some denominations provide their ministers with a service book that contains several options for the wording of the committal service. They will be something like this:

> Inasmuch as our Sovereign Lord has called from this life [name], we do now commit his/her body to the earth from which it came, for we were created from the dust and we return to the dust. We commit his/her soul into the hands of our loving Father and gracious Savior who promised to prepare a place in heaven for all who trust in Him.

You may want to close with a brief Scripture reading, such as Revelation 21:1–5, and then pray. In your prayer, ask the Lord to give the family grace and inner healing as they return to life with its duties. Perhaps the family might want the gathered family and friends to join in the Lord's Prayer. If so, be sure to specify whether "debts" or "trespasses" or "sins" will be used.

After the committal, people usually linger at the graveside and visit, so unless you have a pressing engagement, tarry with them and be available. In some areas, there is a tradition of giving each family member a flower from the casket spray. Often the cemetery staff wants to get on with their work and close up the grave, but an extra five or ten minutes' wait won't ruin their day. The funeral director may invite the mourners to lunch or an afternoon coffee with the family at the church, and he will make that announcement. If the gathering is not at the church but elsewhere, it's wise to have maps available for out-of-town guests. If you can join them at this meal, do so; if not, inform the family member in charge and excuse yourself.

THERE IS SOMETHING LOVING AND STATELY
ABOUT PALLBEARERS CARRYING THE CASKET
TO THE GRAVESIDE AS A FINAL TRIBUTE.

More and more cemeteries now have their own chapels and are encouraging families to have the committal service in the chapel rather than at the graveside. When the weather is bad, this is a convenient option; but we prefer to have the graveside committal because of its finality. When you use the chapel, the mourners never see the casket taken to the grave, and they may wonder when and how it will be done. There is something loving and stately about pallbearers carrying the casket to the graveside as a final act of tribute to their loved one or friend. When we have the committal in the chapel, after the crowd disperses, the casket is taken from the chapel and transported to the grave on a cart pulled by cemetery workers or perhaps by a worker driving a tractor.

It's always proper for the presiding minister to thank the funeral director, the pallbearers, and the musicians for assisting in the service.

AFTER THE FUNERAL AND COMMITTAL

Bereaved people usually need encouragement and assistance for weeks after burying a loved one. Friends mean well when they say, "Call if you need us!" but they soon get back into their own routines and forget their promises. Family members may live hundreds of miles away and can only keep contact by telephone or e-mail. The pastor and the church family must be sensitive to the needs of the bereaved and do what they can to visit personally. Unless there's some deep emotional problem, most mourners eventually go through the healing process successfully.

It's wise for the minister to call in the home soon after the funeral and plan to listen and respond with biblical encouragement. People who "took it so well" at the funeral service have been known to fall apart the next day. The first Sunday the family is back in church worshiping, welcome them publicly and remember them in the pastoral prayer. As you minister to the mourners, be alert for signs of trouble within them and between them. Funerals bring out either the best or the worst in people, and the same crisis that helps one person mature causes another person to become childish and cause trouble. The death of a baby or a little child can put tremendous strain on the marriage and perhaps result in divorce. Don't hesitate to suggest seeking professional help and stay at their side to help them through the crisis. There is such a thing as "extended grief," and it must be dealt with by a professional.

You will sense that the heart is healing when people can speak about the deceased without "going to pieces." This doesn't mean they don't cry, because tears are a normal part of grief, but that they have their feelings under control. It's a great day when they can smile or laugh out loud when recalling something from the past. It's a good sign when they start to accept full responsibility of their lives and use their sorrow as a tool to build with and not a weapon to fight with. "Pastor, I'm just acting like an old fool!" said one elderly widow with a smile, and both the smile and her words signaled that she had turned the corner.

Perhaps abnormal regret is one of the most painful obstacles bereaved people must overcome. "If only I had phoned the doctor sooner!" "Why did we let Junior have the car?" In their minds, they know they can't change the past, and their hearts may be breaking, but they can decide to change their attitudes about the past and start living for the future. We can choose to turn our regrets over to the Lord and to move on with our lives. This is the mature way to act, knowing that one day we will fully understand the will of the Lord. As Jesus said to Peter, "You do not realize now what I am doing, but later you will understand" (John 13:7). Romans 8:28 doesn't say only that everything will work out for good *in the end,* but that everything is working out for good *here and now!* That includes our mistakes and regrets.

People who have buried loved ones sometimes get attached to the calendar and remember meaningful dates, but forget where they parked their car. We recall one dear lady who dated every event in her life from the day her husband died. Parents who have buried a child are also prone to do this. To outsiders this seems tedious and perhaps morbid, but it's their way of keeping the deceased person "alive" in their experience. There's nothing wrong with their saying, "Tommy would have been ten today," or "Dad and Mom would be celebrating their fiftieth anniversary today." But the past must be a rudder to guide us and not an anchor to hold us back. When those "memory days" come—and they will—just advise people to get off by themselves, have a good cry and thank the Lord for the memories of their loved ones, and then go out and do something for somebody. Some families like to place bouquets of flowers in the church sanctuary in memory of deceased loved ones, and this should always be planned in cooperation with the church office. The gesture should be recognized from the pulpit or in the worship folder.

CELEBRATING A LIFE, RECOGNIZING A DEATH

More and more families are holding memorial services to honor the deceased, sometimes following a private committal service. The minister and family of the deceased, with invited friends, meet at the cemetery at, say, nine o'clock in the morning and participate in the committal service. It would be proper for the minister to give an abbreviated message suited to the occasion, and perhaps even some family members or friends present would like to share briefly. If the public service is scheduled at the church for ten o'clock, there should be plenty of time for the trip to the church after the committal service. The family should consider the logistics of the situation and fix the schedule that suits them best.

Since the deceased has already been properly buried, the atmosphere at the memorial service may be a bit more relaxed, but it must not become so laid-back that it turns into a circus. After all, there are people present who hurt deeply, and though we are celebrating a life, we are also recognizing a death. The memorial service must be carefully planned and not left to chance, with selected music, Scripture readings, a eulogy, and a message from the Word of God. But there are other elements that the family may request, such as a video presentation of the deceased person's life and an "open mike" for people to say what's on their hearts. It must be made very clear that those who speak must be brief and not ramble, and what they say must honor the Lord. To adapt a statement from Spurgeon, who was speaking about public prayer: "Some people when they stand to speak grow; others just swell." The memorial service is no place for entertainers.

IT MUST BE MADE VERY CLEAR THAT THOSE
WHO SPEAK MUST BE BRIEF AND NOT RAMBLE,
AND WHAT THEY SAY MUST HONOR THE LORD

After the memorial service, the guests may go to the fellowship hall for any refreshments the family has planned. Most churches have a special committee whose ministry it is to assist in preparing these meals. This post-funeral meal isn't just an occasion to eat and enjoy seeing people we haven't seen in a long time. Primarily, it's a time to affirm Christian love, strengthen Christian fellowship, and encourage the bereaved as they begin their journey toward healing.

IS CREMATION CHRISTIAN?

The English word *cremation* comes from the Latin *cremare,* which means "to burn." It's the process of applying intense heat to the body and casket until all has turned to ashes, technically called "cremains." In the United States in the 1960s, about 3 percent of funerals concluded with the cremation of the body, but that number has risen to about 24 percent today and is expected to reach 50 percent by the year 2025. Some researchers believe that the spread of AIDS has helped fuel this increase. Cremation is the preferred practice in England, where at least 60 percent of the bodies are cremated. Most families opt to have the urn and ashes buried in a cemetery plot, but some families place the urn in a columbarium. A third option is to scatter the ashes at some place that was special to the deceased. It should be noted that you must get local government permission to scatter ashes in public places, such as over a lake or the ocean or in a park.

But is cremation Christian or pagan? For that matter, is embalming a Christian practice? After all, the Egyptians were not Christians, yet they developed the science of embalming to a high degree. Orthodox Jews don't practice either embalming or cremation. According to their law, "burning in the fire" was the punishment assigned to very wicked law-breakers (Leviticus 20:14; 21:9). Joshua 7:24–26 suggests that first the person was stoned and then the body cremated. The bodies of Saul and his sons were burned and their bones buried (1 Samuel 31:8–13), and later David disinterred their remains and buried them in Saul's family tomb (2 Samuel 21:11–14). The Greeks cremated dead soldiers to keep the enemy from abusing their bodies and shaming them. Hindus and Buddhists have practiced cremation for centuries.

Although we know of no biblical teaching that forbids cremation, the evidence in Scripture is overwhelmingly on the side of burial. Abraham, Isaac, Jacob and Joseph (both of whom were embalmed), and subsequent leaders of Israel were all buried, as were the common people, and the Lord buried the body of Moses (Deuteronomy 34:1–8). Christian believers practiced burial of the dead in the New Testament era. In Europe, during plague epidemics, the dead were sometimes cremated for sanitary reasons, but the general practice in Western society has been burial. In 1963, the Roman Catholic Church lifted its ban on cremation and today permits the presence of the ashes at the funeral mass. However, they still prefer burial. The Greek Orthodox Church does not find cremation acceptable.

The pagan Romans used to cremate the dead bodies of Christian martyrs to prevent them from being resurrected, which proves they didn't understand Christian theology. Resurrection is not reconstruction. God doesn't gather the particles and put them back together again. At the resurrection the believer receives a new body that is suited to the new heavenly environment (1 Corinthians 15:35ff.; Philippians 3:20–21). Cremation accomplishes in a few hours what nature does to a buried body over many years: both turn the body to dust.

There are about two hundred crematoriums (or crematoria) in the United States, most of them owned and operated by the boards of local cemeteries, and all of them governed by state and local laws. Some states require the participation of a licensed funeral director for each cremation, and all of them require that the body be placed in "a suitable container" for the cremation process. As far as we know, there is no law that demands the body be placed in an expensive casket. However, if there is to be a public viewing of the body before cremation, there must be a casket and the body must be embalmed. There was a time when cremation was much more economical than traditional burial, but that day is over.

> RESURRECTION IS NOT RECONSTRUCTION.
> GOD DOESN'T GATHER THE PARTICLES
> AND PUT THEM BACK TOGETHER AGAIN.

What part does the minister play in a funeral that involves the cremating of the deceased? In most instances, there is usually a traditional funeral service first. It may be held at the church, at the funeral home, or in a cemetery chapel near the crematorium. When the service is over, the funeral director will transport the body to the crematorium. From that time, there are several options open, but in most cases, the interment of the cremains is at a later time.

If the ashes are to be buried in the cemetery, the family may want a traditional committal service at the grave, so you will have to work out the schedule with them. It takes between two and three hours to complete the cremation process, and you may not have the time to sit around and wait. If the urn is to be placed in a columbarium, the family might want a brief, informal committal service. Many crematoriums have a special room called "the committal chamber" where the pastor and family may meet and have a brief service before the cremation begins. The minister doesn't have to be present for the cremation process or at the time when the urn is given to the family. However the family plans it, the faithful shepherd is there to be of help and should be sensitive to their needs.

What does the minister say at a cremation service? For one thing, we don't use vivid Scriptures that refer to fire! The focus is on mortality, the divine decree found in Genesis 3:17–19, and other verses such as Job 7:21; 10:9; 17:16; 20:11; 21:26; 34:15; Psalms 7:5; 22:15; 90:3; 104:29; Ecclesiastes 3:20; 12:7; Isaiah 26:19 (which also mentions resurrection); and Daniel 12:2 (another resurrection verse). But mortality must be balanced by immortality (1 Corinthians 15:53–54; 1 Timothy 1:17; 6:16;

2 Timothy 1:10). Dust and ashes are not the end! Yes, God knows that we are but dust (Psalm 103:14), but He is eternal and welcomes His children to heaven when they pass from this life.

MILITARY AND FRATERNAL SERVICES

It isn't likely that most of us will participate in a formal military funeral with a chapel service, a military band, a march to the gravesite, and the required music and salutes. If you are so honored, talk to the presiding chaplain and find out what you are supposed to do. There are still many loyal veterans who want to be recognized in death as well as life, and they have every right to be so. This means enlisting other veterans to assist you at the burial, and this may be difficult. However, the family can help you, as can the veterans' organization of which the deceased was a member. Even if he or she didn't belong to an official group, you will find the local veterans more than willing to assist.

The minister follows the usual liturgy at the graveside, concluding with the committal and benediction, and then the veterans take over. However, if the family desires, the military part can come first and the committal follow. Depending on the number and skills of the veterans available, there is usually a formal rifle salute, the playing of taps, and the folding and presenting of the flag to the nearest of kin. Once this is done, the funeral director will announce that the graveside services are completed and the people may go to their vehicles.

As for the fraternal services, ministers and churches have different convictions and practices. Some ministers will have nothing to do with fraternal orders, feeling that if they do they will compromise their Christian convictions, while others may belong to a lodge personally and make no apology for it. If lodge membership is an issue in the church, the minister should discuss it with the official board privately early in his ministry at that church and not wait until the first fraternal funeral comes along. The congregation and the lodge members should respect the pastor's convictions, but the pastor must not try to force his convictions on others. "Do not allow what you consider good to be spoken of as evil" (Romans 14:16).

Our experience has been that most chaplains in fraternal orders are understanding and cooperative and have no desire to create problems. If there is to be a formal fraternal ceremony, the chaplain may ask to have it at the funeral home the evening before the funeral, usually at the close of the wake, or they may prefer to conduct it the next day before the funeral itself. Courtesy isn't necessarily compromise. The Christian witness of the deceased should be of greater importance to the family than any other commitment, but sometimes people's values get confused. "If it is possible, as far as it depends on you, live at peace with everyone" (Romans 12:18). The wise and loving shepherd knows what to say and when to be silent, when to stand firm and when to cooperate graciously. To quote Charles Spurgeon again, sometimes it's best for the minister to have "one blind eye and one deaf ear" than to create a problem that would cripple his future ministry. "Each [man] should be fully convinced in his own mind" (Romans 14:5).

Notes

1. Jessica Mitford, *The American Way of Death Revisited* (New York: Knopf, 1998), 17.

2. Quoted in Laderman, *Rest in Peace: A Cultural History of Death and the Funeral Home in Twentieth-Century America* (New York: Oxford University Press, 2003), 110–11.

3. *New York Times,* April 14, 2002, "Week in Review" section, p. 3.

Challenging Situations

"Everybody at the funeral knew that my husband had committed suicide, but the preacher said nothing about it," said one sorrowing wife. "How come?"

While most of the funerals we conduct will be of the "normal" variety, occasionally we will have to preside at "crisis" funerals that present special challenges—a healthy baby died unexpectedly, a teenager was killed in an accident, a young mother was murdered, a man committed suicide. We live in a dangerous world, and anything is liable to happen at any time.

As ministers and caregivers, we can take one of three approaches to these special situations. We can *ignore* the unique—and tragic—elements completely and carry on as though nothing unusual has happened, hoping that something we say will meet the need. But, as the sorrowing wife's lament above attests, to overlook such a tragedy can only compound the grief.

The second approach swings to the other extreme: the minister tries to *explain* why things happened as they did and throws in a few Bible verses to make his analysis "official." That's the approach Job's friends took. It didn't work then, and it doesn't work now. To begin with, only God knows why things happen as they do and why people do what they do, and it's dangerous for us to "play God." But even more, *people don't live on explanations; they live on promises.* Knowing why the plane crashed or the bleachers collapsed doesn't bring much comfort, but using the promises in Scriptures to bring Jesus Christ close to hurting people will encourage the healing process. "Why, Lord?" is an easy question to ask; but He doesn't always give us immediate answers.[1]

The third approach is the wisest one: *interpret events and feelings in the light of the Word of God,* as Jesus did for the two bewildered men on the road to Emmaus (Luke 24). People don't need better reasons; they need better relationships with the Lord and with others, and that comes from the Holy Spirit applying the Word. Confused and angry people have to face reality, accept it, and trust God to give them strength for the days ahead. "The secret things belong to the Lord our God, but the things revealed belong to us and to our sons forever, that we may observe all the words of this law" (Deuteronomy 29:29 NASB). Obeying what God has already told us often leads to discovering the hidden things He wants us to know (John 7:17).

The funeral message must be a "catalyst" that reflects the feelings of the listeners and offers the help God can give them as they go through their dark valley. There are no instant remedies; if they give God time, He will heal their hurts. They must "imitate those who through faith and patience inherit what has been promised" (Hebrews 6:12). A truly biblical message puts a painful situation into a larger God-centered context and presents the perspective of eternity. Seeing Jesus Christ by faith is the answer to every basic question of life, and that's what biblical preaching is all about. The minister doesn't give pat answers or quote theological explanations from learned authorities. There will be time enough in the days to come for us to answer the questions hurting people ask, but for now, we major on the glory of Christ and the gracious promises of God.

One word of caution: Jesus made it clear that tragedies aren't always the consequences of somebody's specific sins (Luke 13:1–9). The worshipers whom Pilate killed in the temple and the eighteen people on whom the tower fell were not greater sinners than anybody else in Jerusalem, yet they died in tragic ways. Our job isn't to try to explain those deaths but to examine our own hearts and repent of our own sins.

In the parable that followed (vv. 6–9), Jesus taught that the major issue isn't "Why did other people die?" but "What right do I have to keep on living? Am I bearing fruit for the Lord?" This passage can be adapted for a funeral message.

THE FUNERAL OF A STRANGER

Those who minister in larger communities are often called upon to conduct funerals for people who are strangers to them and to their congregations. When funeral directors find willing pastors with compassionate hearts, they add them to their unofficial staff and ask for their assistance when they need it. Don't be offended at this. Conducting the funeral of a stranger is an opportunity to meet other strangers and minister to them, and who knows what the Lord might accomplish? The Old Testament law commanded the Israelites to be kind to strangers (Exodus 22:21; Leviticus 19:34; Deuteronomy 27:19). When Jesus healed the ten lepers, it was the "stranger"—the Samaritan—who returned to thank Him, and he received the gift of salvation (Luke 17:11–19). "I was a stranger and you invited me in" (Matthew 25:35).

Talk to the funeral director and learn all you can about the deceased. If there is a visitation time, you should be there to meet family (if any) and friends and get as much information as you can. Don't act like an inquiring reporter, pen and notebook in hand. Instead, be a concerned shepherd who ministers to the mourners. There are ways of innocently responding to what people say that will encourage them to say more, but don't accept all they say at face value. Most people don't like to speak evil of the dead, and hidden guilt sometimes motivates people to exaggerate the good points.

Chat with the family member or friend who is in charge of the arrangements and find out what kind of funeral service is expected. Perhaps the deceased left directions concerning the service and burial or may have discussed it with somebody during those final days. Does the doctor know anything about it, or the lawyer who drew up the will? A busy pastor can't spend a great deal of time playing detective, but the more we know, the better we are able to minister. Even then, somebody will probably say, "Just do whatever is supposed to be done—and make it short!"

To open the service with "I never met John Doe, so I don't know much about him" is to ask the congregation to stop listening. The word *stranger* must not be used. (God knows no strangers.) On the other hand, to say "I feel like I knew John" would be deceitful. Let's face it: the assembled family and friends know that you were invited to be there and that you're ministering under some handicaps. They invited you because they wanted the deceased to be buried with dignity, so don't disappoint them. Be authentic, be compassionate, and represent the Savior.

> TO OPEN THE SERVICE WITH 'I NEVER MET JOHN DOE, SO I DON'T KNOW MUCH ABOUT HIM' IS TO ASK THE CONGREGATION TO STOP LISTENING.

If you can open the message with some point of contact with the deceased or the family, by all means do so. This will help to get their attention, and they may decide that you're worth listening to after all, so launch into the service before they change their minds! The service should be brief, but not hurried, and made as personal as possible in spite of the circumstances. Once you have built the bridge, you can use the message to share the love of Christ with them. Your opportunities for deeper ministry may come weeks later.

THE "WICKED SINNER"

During the Victorian era in England, a man named John Starkey murdered his wife and was tried, found guilty, and executed. The authorities asked General William Booth, founder of the Salvation Army, to preach the funeral sermon, and he faced that day a congregation of hard-hearted sinners who had little regard for God's law or the law of the land. Booth opened the sermon by saying, "John Starkey did not have a praying mother!" Many of the men in the congregation *did* have praying mothers who loved them, and Booth's statement hit home.

We aren't likely to have that same experience, but we can learn from Booth's strategy. He didn't try to preach John Starkey into heaven—although nobody knows what eternal transactions Starkey may have made before he died—but Booth did begin with a statement that arrested their attention and touched their hearts.

Who are these "wicked sinners"? Many smaller communities and metropolitan neighborhoods have persons who are proud to be known for their defiance of God, morality, and even common sense. We recall a man saying, "If this floor opened up and I dropped into hell right now, it wouldn't bother me one bit." By God's grace, that man lived long enough to receive Christ and have the assurance of heaven. Some of these so-called outsiders may be the relatives or friends of reputable church members somewhere, people who are praying for them. Let's help answer those prayers.

Here's another William Booth story, told by his son Bramwell in his autobiography *Echoes and Memories*. When Bramwell was in his early teens, he and his father were walking past a public house in London when Booth suddenly led his son into the place. The room reeked of tobacco and alcohol and was crowded with noisy, dirty people, some of whom were drunk. Father and son gazed at the tragic scene, and then Booth said, "Willie, these are our people. These are the people I want you to live for and bring to Christ." Bramwell Booth added in his book, "The impression never left me."

No matter how stained may be the deceased person's record, we who minister must be like Jesus and manifest love and acceptance, despising the sin but not the sinner.

Our task is to be a witness for Christ and not a prosecuting attorney. We don't whitewash the past or exaggerate the future, but we do "speak the truth in love" to those left behind. Let's speak less about the deceased and more about the Savior who was the friend of sinners.

Psalm 81 may help us reach some hearts. In the first ten verses, Asaph reminds us of the goodness of the Lord, the blessings people enjoy whether they acknowledge God or not. In the last six verses, Asaph laments over all that the people might have enjoyed if they had listened to God. "The things that might have been" is a sobering theme. However, for those listening to us, "what might have been" *may still be*, if hearts will open to the Lord by faith. We can't change the past, but we can make decisions that will change the future.

Texts like Matthew 7:21–23 and 8:11–12 warn us that some who expect to go to heaven won't be there, while some we don't expect to see will be there. Jesus taught this lesson to Simon the Pharisee (Luke 7:36–50), and people need to learn it today. Simon didn't see the truth about the woman because he didn't even face the truth about himself! Our task isn't to pass judgment on the dead but to press the claims of Jesus Christ on the hearts of the living.

We must never forget the thief on the cross (Luke 23:39–43) who seized, not his last opportunity to be saved, but his *first* opportunity. There's no evidence that he had met Jesus before or heard Him speak, and the only way he found out that Jesus had a kingdom was from Pilate's sign placed above our Lord's head: "This is Jesus of Nazareth, the King of the Jews." He heard the mockers say, "He saved others," and this may have encouraged him to ask for help. This thief does not encourage people to wait until the very end to trust Jesus, but to trust Him the first time they meet Him! There are no guarantees that everybody will have an opportunity for a last-minute conversion, but the thief does encourage us that such miracles do happen. Our message might be based on a familiar "salvation" text like John 3:16, the Parable of the Prodigal Son, Paul's testimony in 1 Timothy 1:15, or David's cry for mercy in Psalm 51.

THE "GOOD, MORAL PERSON"

But not all lost sinners are of the variety we have just discussed. Good, moral people are just as lost as the worst man or woman in town. Good, moral people aren't outcasts, just outsiders, happy-go-lucky, successful people who are friendly neighbors and good citizens, but who don't see the need for God or "religion." They take care of their families materially but are impervious to all appeals to attend church or think about God. They are "secular people" who never apologize for leaving God out of their lives, and everybody knows where they stand. Then they die, and custom dictates that they have a decent burial. What will the minister say about the "good, moral person" who never had an enemy but lived at enmity with God?

The publicans and sinners whom Jesus befriended (Matthew 11:19; Luke 15:1–2) probably fit into this category. They were Jews who ignored their spiritual heritage and didn't attend the synagogue or celebrate the holy days at the temple. Jesus saw them as lost sheep, lost coins, and rebellious children (Luke 15), as well as patients suffering from sin sickness and desperately needing the help of a compassionate physician (Matthew 9:9–12). Jesus was criticized for eating with these people, but converts like Matthew and Zacchaeus are evidence that His ministry wasn't wasted. Saul of Tarsus was a good, moral sinner until Jesus knocked him off his "high horse" and revealed Himself to him.

In today's relativistic and pluralistic society it's difficult to find people who admit they are sinners, for one lifestyle is as acceptable as another. But the Bible assures us that sinners are still with us. We can certainly be thankful for people who do good works for their family and community, even though we know that these works will never earn them a place in heaven. Cornelius did good works, even religious works, and this eventually led to his salvation through faith in Christ (Acts 10). Only the Lord can convict the heart of self-righteous and self-satisfied moral sinners and make them realize that their righteousness is but filthy rags in the sight of the Lord.

It's interesting to contrast the descriptions of Job in Job 1:1–3, 8 with what he said about himself in Job 40:3–5 and 42:6. Once Job beheld God in His holiness, his attitude was changed, and all his arguments were destroyed. He joined the ranks of the many people described in the Bible whose mouths were shut because they were convicted of their sins (Romans 3:19). Or, we might consider our Lord's parable about the two men praying in the temple (Luke 18:9–14), or Paul's autobiography in Philippians 3:4–11. It takes some homiletical skill to package these texts in such a way that our listeners will understand and apply them, but it can be done. Saul of Tarsus was a "successful failure" who needed to meet Jesus Christ, and so is every "good, moral person" who has never trusted Christ.

MULTIPLE DEATHS

We usually think of air transportation as the major cause of multiple deaths in a family, but modern ground transportation is merciless when it gets out of control, and you don't have to be in a vehicle to be killed. Just follow the news. A careless or drunken driver swerves into a crowd and kills a mother and daughter who are shopping. A runaway truck smashes through a restaurant window and kills a husband and wife enjoying a birthday lunch.

One of our earliest funerals was for a mother and her young daughter who were burned to death in a kitchen fire. Perhaps the most difficult service was for a father, mother, and young son. The father had shot his wife and son and then killed himself.

AT TIMES OF TRAGEDY, A PASTOR WHO
LEANS ON PIOUS PLATITUDES WILL
SEND PEOPLE AWAY HUNGRY.

At times like these, the minister who leans on sentimental poetry and pious platitudes is sure to fail and send people away hungry. We must help the mourners face reality, accept the pain and perplexity of all that has happened, and turn to Christ for the help only He can give. In the days that follow, we must take time for personal counseling and try to answer questions so the mourners can work their way through anger, confusion, and vindictive feelings. At times of tragedy, a pastor who leans on pious platitudes will send people away hungry.

"And the two of them went on together" (Genesis 22:8) describes a father and son going up to meet God on the mountain, and Ruth 1:16–17 is the testimony of a daughter-in-law to her mother-in-law, but both texts can be adapted and applied to other family members. In 2 Samuel 1, David lamented the deaths of a father and a beloved son, and in Matthew 2:13–18, you have the inhuman slaughter of innocent children by an evil man.

In some funerals involving multiple deaths, a different family member or friend might give a short tribute for the deceased. In this way, the funeral is made personal and the minister can focus on the preaching of the Word.

Let's not waste time with useless explaining; instead, let's assure the mourners that God has not abandoned them and that one day we shall fully understand. Meanwhile, they must return to life with its burdens and opportunities and seek to bring comfort to others. Truths from Luke 13:1–9 can also be applied to these difficult situations. Seek the Lord, take time to pray and quiet your heart, immerse yourself in the Word, and the Holy Spirit will teach you what to say. He is the Comforter.

Multiple death situations and murders usually draw the press, because their job is to keep the public informed, and reporters have a right to earn an honest living. They may approach you for a statement, but try to keep them at bay until your own preparation is completed or, better yet, until after the funeral. If you have a wise secretary or assistant, let him or her help to shield you. A reporter may show up at the funeral and take notes on your message, so don't preach yourself into a libel suit. As we've said before, we are witnesses and not prosecuting attorneys. "Let your conversation be always full of grace . . ." (Colossians 4:6).

THE MURDER VICTIM

There was a time when the average minister rarely had a funeral service for a person who was the victim of foul play, but things have changed. In these days of violence and more accessible firearms—even to children—anything can happen. One would think that a day care center or a grade school would be the safest place in town, but even they have seen their share of brutality and bullets. We can all say with David, "There is only a step between me and death" (1 Samuel 20:3).

A funeral service is not the place for a theological discussion about the providence of God or the problem of evil in the world. We can take care of that kind of instruction during the regular course of our pulpit ministry. Ever since the fall of our first parents, this world has been in bondage to sin, so we aren't surprised at reports of famines, earthquakes, airplane crashes, automobile accidents, and senseless violence. We have already mentioned the way Jesus handled reports of tragedies in His day (Luke 13:1–9), pointing out that the main question isn't, "Why did they die?" but "What right do *we* have to be alive?"

"Where was the Lord when all this violence occurred?" is the normal question stunned people ask, and the answer is, "The same place He was when His own Son was treated so violently and then crucified—God was on the throne of the universe." (See Acts 2:23; 3:15.) The next question is usually, "Why didn't He do something to prevent it?" We could spend hours seeking answers to that question, but essentially the answer is wrapped up in the word *freedom*. We are free to make decisions and even to make mistakes, and this means we may suffer from the bad decisions other people make. When we arrive in heaven, we will probably learn how many times God and His angels intervened on our behalf when we were heading for trouble.

King Solomon pondered the problems of evil in this world (Ecclesiastes 3:16–17; 4:1–3) and came to the pessimistic conclusion that it would be better not to be born! But Paul reminds us that God's goal for His children is that they be "conformed to the likeness of his Son" (Romans 8:29), and that makes life worthwhile. If the Son of God experienced violence, suffering, and even death while ministering on earth, why should we be exempted? If we depend on the grace of God, suffering can build character (2 Corinthians 12:1–10); but if God intervened every time we were about to be in danger, we would never develop Christian character. Jesus "learned obedience from what he suffered" (Hebrews 5:8), and so must we. Our Lord's sufferings eventually turned into glory, and so will ours. The wicked seem to be prospering in this world, but the day of reckoning will come.

While they were crucifying Jesus, He prayed, "Father, forgive them, for they do not know what they are doing" (Luke 23:34), and that must be our attitude toward those who do evil against us and our loved ones. David in Psalm 11 vividly describes the situation: the enemy is shooting at the just, the just feel like flying away from it all, and the very foundations of morality and peace are shaking. But God is still on the throne and sees what's going on, and we can trust Him to do what is right.

The prophet Habakkuk saw terrible violence in his own day and cried out for God to act (Habakkuk 1:1–4). But the Lord responded in chapter 2 by giving him three wonderful assurances: God's people live by faith (v. 4), God's glory will ultimately triumph (v. 14), and God is on His throne doing what is right (v. 20). In chapter 3, the prophet leaves it all with the Lord and triumphs by worshiping and trusting. Habakkuk 3:17–19 records one of the greatest confessions of faith found anywhere in the Bible. It can be our confession of faith if we yield to the Lord and depend on Him. "Though the fig tree does not bud and there are no grapes on the vines, though the olive crop fails and the fields produce no food, though there are no sheep in the pen and no cattle in the stalls, yet I will rejoice in the LORD, I will be joyful in God my Savior. The Sovereign LORD is my strength; he makes my feet like the feet of a deer, he enables me to go on the heights."

A FUNERAL WITHOUT THE BODY OF THE DECEASED

Sometimes it's a military man or woman lost in battle, or a drowning victim whose body was never recovered, or the victim of a mass tragedy like the Twin Towers 9/11 attack. This kind of funeral service is especially difficult, because the mourners cannot make that final confrontation with the deceased and therefore may not accept the fact that their loved one is really dead. There will be pictures on display, perhaps even personal belongings that remind everybody of the deceased, but the difficulty of "closure" leaves a huge vacuum in some people's hearts.

You prepare as you would for a memorial service that would follow the interment of the body. The remains may be absent, but God is still present, and His promises are still valid. Deal compassionately with the feelings people have because of the tragedy. The Lord knows how they feel about the absence of their loved one, and He knows where the loved one's remains are resting. Psalm 139:1–12 reminds us that God knows everything about the deceased *and about us.* The prayer in verses 23–24 is applicable to all of us.

"Now we see but a poor reflection as in a mirror; then we shall see face to face" (1 Corinthians 13:12). We don't enjoy the "now" but we can anticipate the "then." The loved ones of Moses saw him before he ascended Mount Nebo, but they couldn't attend his funeral because God buried him (Deuteronomy 34). If the mourners had seen the deceased alive before the tragedy occurred and the remains were lost, the situation would be easier to accept; but we cannot change the past, and it's not wise to second-guess the Lord.

In the weeks that follow, you may have to do some patient personal work with some of the mourners and help them work through their anger, bewilderment, unbelief, or whatever other feelings may have captured them. Since there is no gravesite to memorialize the deceased, you may want to suggest a "living memorial" to assist others in their needs, a gift to a children's hospital or a veterans' organization. There are other people who are also mourning their losses.

THE FUNERAL OF A CHILD OR YOUTH

The visitation for a child is usually crowded, because hearts respond with compassion when a child or an adolescent dies. In some communities, school is dismissed so the students can attend the funeral, and it isn't unusual for the school gymnasium to become the sanctuary for the service of a popular student. A child's death means that something is out of sync in the universe—but God is still on His throne.

> A CHILD'S DEATH MEANS THAT SOMETHING IS
>
> OUT OF SYNC IN THE UNIVERSE—
>
> BUT GOD IS STILL ON HIS THRONE.

In both of these situations, the service must have its own special atmosphere. For the child, it is tenderness, simplicity, the calmness of the lullaby, the soft breath of the nursery—and not the strong wind of a lecture room. For the adolescent, it depends on the interests and accomplishments of the deceased: athletics, art, music, academics, student government. Let's not settle for a "generic funeral."

At the start of the service for a child, the leader should confess that a child's death means that something is out of sync in the universe, but that God is still on His throne. In God's garden (see 1 Corinthians 15:35–50) there are all kinds of plants, and sometimes He plucks the youngest and smallest for His garden above (Song of Solomon 6:2). Since heaven is a place of completion and perfection, we believe that children grow up in heaven and that Christian parents will know their deceased children and their children will know them. Each winter we see the flowers and trees "die," and each spring we see the new life displayed in beauty. This is God's way, and we can trust Him.

The family may want to include some of the child's favorite music, and this is fine so long as it fits into the funeral naturally. Otherwise, perhaps it could be played at the fellowship meal following the interment. It would not be out of place to display some of the child's toys or favorite photographs.

The account of David and the death of his child by Bathsheba (2 Samuel 12:15–23) contains one of the finest promises for grieving parents (v. 23), but the details that precede verse 23 may not be suitable for a funeral message. Will the parents erroneously conclude that their child died because they sinned? First Corinthians 13:11–13 contrasts child-hood and maturity in spiritual things, but it also suggests that a time is coming when we will see God and understand His works even as He sees and understands us.

The committal service for a child has to be the most difficult part of the day for the parents and siblings as they see the little casket placed into the ground. It may help if everybody present sang a children's song, such as "Jesus Loves Me" or "Jesus Loves the Little Children" or even the famil-iar "Luther's Cradle Hymn" ("Away in a Manger"). Stay close to the family after the committal and make frequent visits to the home in the weeks that follow. See the appendix for suggestions for messages for the funeral of a child.

Sometimes the mother is still in the hospital or recovering at home and is unable to attend the funeral service. She will not see the baby in the casket, and this could make closure difficult, so be alert to signs of distress. When a newborn baby dies, many hospitals wisely move the mother to a different part of the building so she won't be upset by the presence of babies, but one day she must go home to the empty crib and be able to deal with the pain of saying good-bye.

And don't forget the father. In the weeks to come, as he returns to his employment, he has many things he must do, and these distractions may help him cope more easily. His stoical attitude may just be his way of cov-ering up his real feelings. Eventually he must handle these feelings ma-turely, so be patient and prayerful. He will be especially concerned for his wife, so encourage them to minister to each other and help each other heal.

If there are other children in the home, they will need special atten-tion, and the parents must never treat them as substitutes for the deceased baby. Children from ages one to five tend to deny the reality of death—the entire experience is unreal to them. They watch their parents joyfully pre-pare for the arrival of the new baby, and then the joy is suddenly replaced by sorrow. The children have seen people "die" in television cartoons and movies, but they don't take it seriously. From ages five to nine, children understand the reality and pain of death but don't quite see how it fits into the scheme of life. They wonder how soon it will happen to them. A child's grief at the loss of a sibling (or a parent) is just as real as that of an adult, though expressed in a more juvenile fashion. Take their grief seriously and help them work their way through it. "This is just a dream" is one defense mechanism, and anger is another—"Why did Daddy do this to us!" A child's world depends on the protection and provision supplied by adults, and when one parent is taken, their world falls apart.

We recall one ten-year-old girl whose father had committed suicide. She wasn't told the truth until a few days after the funeral. The widow asked her pastor to "explain it to her," and he did his best. The girl's first question was, "Didn't he love us?" At that point, the pastor began to weep, and his tears, more than anything else, assured the girl that God really cared for her. They quoted Psalm 23 together, prayed together, and "made a date" to meet again. It wasn't easy, but it was the beginning of healing for her.

The child who expresses no emotion may be the one who needs more help. Children must not be forced to grieve, but they must be free to grieve in their own way and at their own pace. "I'm not going to cry because it just makes Mommy cry" is a brave attitude, but if the child wept *with* Mommy and Daddy, it would do all of them more good. It's easy to say, "Be brave," but it's also good to say, "Be human." To shelter maturing children from the painful realities of life is cruel. Instead, let's show and teach them how to accept life, and let's not try to explain everything. They must honestly express their emotions in the atmosphere of love that we help to create in the home.

Children look to the adults in their lives for the explanations they need, and we can't always answer their questions. Let's admit it and give them some of God's promises to hold to. Don't try to explain beyond their level of comprehension or, for that matter, beyond our own level of understanding and experience. We don't have to play God, but we do have to try to lead them closer to God, and we do that by being our very best self with His help.

IT'S EASY TO SAY 'BE BRAVE,'
BUT IT'S ALSO GOOD TO SAY, 'BE HUMAN.'

In the days following the funeral, it's important that the family read the Bible together and pray together, as though the deceased child were still with them. The children should be taught that their sibling is alive in heaven and that there are still three children in the family—"two on earth and one in heaven." In your postfuneral ministry, you will want to spend time with all the family and schedule special times with the parents. Ask the children to share their happiest memories about their brother or sister. Some families recognize the deceased child's birthday each year, but this must not become a "pseudocelebration" or an occasion for opening wounds that the Lord has healed.

Now let's consider the funeral of a youth. Young people think that they are invincible and will live on earth and "have fun" forever, and the death of a peer is a sobering shock. Teenagers see a great deal of death on television and in movies, but since these events are fundamentally for entertainment, the young people don't take it too seriously. So when a friend dies, many teenagers don't know what to say or how to act. They may adopt a temporary stoicism to cover up their real feelings. After all, real men don't cry. If the deceased was an avowed Christian and a part of the church family, this makes our task much easier at the funeral.

The real problems appear when the deceased died because of some foolish action or because he or she was in the wrong place with the wrong people. Driving while drunk, speeding on a gravel road, taking a stupid dare, playing with the famous gun that is never loaded, getting involved in a gang rumble—any of these can spell death. The funeral message, however, isn't for the deceased teenager but for the living teenagers and adults who need to be reminded that life is precious, death is no respecter of persons, and Jesus wants to be Savior and Master of their lives. Don't emphasize the negative and add to the burdens the family is already carrying. The body in the casket is preaching its own sermon very clearly, and the young person's absence will continue preaching for months to come. Introduce people to Jesus and He will do the rest.

It isn't out of place for some of the peers of the deceased to express themselves briefly at the funeral. It's best that they write out their contribution and read it rather than speak extemporaneously. Nor is it out of place to display trophies or other awards or to hear from adults who knew the deceased teenager. All of this can be overdone, so in our planning we must be careful not to praise the dead teenager so much that we ignore the living Christ. And let's not forget the parents and grandparents who helped to make the teenager what he or she was.

THE FUNERAL OF A SUICIDE[2]

To admit or not to admit? That is the question. If the official verdict by the doctor and the coroner is "suicide," then people will probably know about it, and there's no reason to cover things up. However, this doesn't give us the license to share the news from the housetops. In fact, we don't need to use the word "suicide" at the funeral or the memorial service. "What has happened is tragic, and we all feel it," says the minister. "It should not have happened, but it *has* happened, and we must accept it. We can't change the past; in fact, we may not fully understand the past. We are not here to pass judgment; we are here to recognize a life, not analyze a death. We are here to seek the Lord and His grace so that we might better understand ourselves, our own lives, and our wonderful Lord."

In the funeral message, we must be sensitive interpreters who apply biblical insights to a difficult situation, and we will seek to avoid simplistic explanations. It's our belief that salvation is by faith and that those who have sincerely trusted Jesus and given valid witness of their faith have received eternal life and the transaction is complete. There was a time when all suicides were considered hopelessly lost, and their remains could not even be buried in the consecrated ground of a cemetery. Thankfully, those days are about over. The people we address at the service are shocked, grieved, weary, perplexed, and no doubt feeling guilty, and our task is to apply the medicine of God's truth to their hearts. "He sent forth his word and healed them" (Psalm 107:20).

King Saul of Israel was guilty of many sins, the last of which was taking his own life; but David was able to say good things about him in his "Song of the Bow" (2 Samuel 1:17–27). The funeral message should focus on the good points of a person's life, the things Paul wrote about in Philippians 4:8. The fact that the deceased took his or her own life need not overshadow the lasting contributions made by that life.

Let's open the service on a positive note by quoting or reading Psalm 86:5, 15—"You are forgiving and good, O Lord, abounding in love to all who call to you. . . . But you, O Lord, are a compassionate and gracious

God, slow to anger, abounding in love and faithfulness." Another option is the more familiar Romans 8:38–39.

Dr. Karl Menninger, the eminent American psychiatrist, has written that "suicide is a very complex act," and pastoral experience tells us that those who mourn over a suicide's death have a tough time and their grief work is especially difficult; so let's not add to their feeling of guilt or helplessness. We should major on the spiritual resources found in Jesus Christ. In the pastoral prayer, we help the congregation seek the Lord's forgiveness. "Father, help us to face honestly the fact of death. Forgive us for the things we should have done for others but failed to do. Too often we have been blind to hurts and needs of others, and we ask for Your forgiveness. We also ask for a loving and sensitive spirit so that we might help others bear their burdens with faith and courage. We cannot change the past, but by Your Spirit, make us more like Jesus in the days to come."

Carefully read all of the verses of any songs that will be sung, lest there be a line or a phrase that could bring embarrassment to the family. Also, be careful in your praying that you don't say something to the Lord that somebody at the service might misunderstand. "We thank You, Lord, that [decedent's name] is now at home with You" is tantamount to saying you are glad the person took his or her own life, and that's not what you mean at all.

See the appendix of this book for suggestions for funeral messages.

DIVIDED FAMILIES

It's a fundamental law of life that a crisis will bring out either the very best in people or the very worst, depending on their character. The same sun that melts the ice will harden the clay. This explains why grieving people who ought to be loving each other and sharing comfort are too often ignoring or even irritating each other. Family divisions often have long histories and deep roots, and we will not fully understand them or be able to remove them with one brief funeral message. But perhaps we can plant some seeds and water them in future pastoral ministry and eventually see some peaceful fruit.

Divorces divide families and complicate relationships. We recall one funeral service to which three different sets of wives and children came to pay their respects to the deceased husband and father. In these situations, the big question isn't, "Whose husband will he be in the resurrection?" but "What can we say to help these people find salvation in Jesus Christ?"

In today's pluralistic society you will also find families divided over their religious faith, and each household wants to follow the customs most familiar to them. But unless you want confusion, you can't plan a funeral on the basis of ecumenical consensus, so the person who invited you to lead the service is the one to listen to. We have sometimes opened a funeral service taking this approach:

> Death has visited your family. Death is called "the great leveler," because it puts all of us on the same level. Death pays no attention to age, income, education, race, religion, or occupation. There is no such thing as Protestant death, Roman Catholic death, Orthodox death, or Jewish death. Death is death. Rich people die as do poor people, and both rich and poor take nothing with them when they leave us. The Bible tells us that people are "destined to die once, and after that to face judgment" (Hebrews 9:27). That includes all of us. Whatever differences may exist among us must be put aside, for death is the great leveler and is no respecter of persons. All of us need the help of the Lord at this time, so let's pause to pray.

After this or a similar introduction, you can proceed with the service. At the committal service, you might say—

> We have been united today because of death, but we are also united in life. God has graciously given us more time to live, to love one another, to serve, and to prepare to meet the Lord. We all came from the dust, and we shall return to the dust. What we do in between is what determines what God will do with us.

You may then continue with the committal service.

Where there are divided families, it's important that we get accurate information about the deceased. One part of the family may paint a beautiful picture, while the other part is throwing mud, or they may get together and agree on a lie. A pastor new to the community was asked to conduct the funeral for a man who was "father" to two families, his own biological children and his second wife's children. After chatting with both families, the pastor thought he had the right view of things and tailored the message accordingly. A few weeks after the service, a relative who had not attended the family planning meeting informed him that the deceased had a very shameful past and had been the cause of endless

---

ONE PART OF THE FAMILY MAY PAINT

A BEAUTIFUL PICTURE OF THE DECEASED—

WHILE THE OTHER PART IS THROWING MUD.

---

trouble to both families. Had the new pastor asked the children, "How do you see this man's life?" instead of merely saying, "Tell me about your father," he might have gotten the right information. He could also have talked with church members who had deep roots in that community, and they would have clued him in.

DEATH IN ANOTHER CONGREGATION

It is our conviction that no minister should conduct the funeral service of a member of another congregation unless the pastor of that congregation knows and approves.

The family members in charge should convey their desires to their pastor, get official approval, and then speak to you. It would be best if both pastors shared in the service, and you might want to make that suggestion. Many churches now have a policy of requiring their pastor or a staff member to participate in weddings and funerals conducted in church facilities for their members, and we think this is a good rule.

Which raises the question, why would people from another congregation want a different shepherd to lay them to rest? If their pastor is out of town, he has no doubt asked a friend in ministry to cover for him in his absence. If the request is simply a matter of personal preference ("We love our pastor, but he doesn't know how to bring comfort at funerals"), then we must be very cautious not to promote schism and what A. W. Tozer used to call "the fan club mentality." In almost every community there are "religious nomads," people who move from church to church looking for the "best expositor" or the "most loving pastor." Their usual reason (or excuse) for asking for your services is that their pastor "doesn't care for them" and has refused to minister to them.

But there may be two sides to that familiar story. It's likely that their pastor understands the family *too* well and has discovered they have a desire to control him and the church. We certainly don't want to encourage that kind of unbiblical practice by conducting a service for somebody we hardly know, especially a person who has created problems for a fellow minister. If the deceased had previously asked for our services, we should be available, but we should share the pulpit with the other pastor and bear witness that we are laborers together with God.

At the beginning of a ministry in a church, godly pastors should let their leaders and members know that they will not serve in weddings or funerals for members of other churches unless that church's pastor is also participating, and the word will get out. No minister of the gospel wants to get the reputation of being a "hireling" who is available for any and all spiritual ministries—at a price.

But perhaps there are exceptions. What if the pastor of the deceased person's church is liberal in theology, or the "church" is really an unbiblical cult, and the true believers in the family want the Word preached in purity? Perhaps the member of the family in charge belongs to your flock, and the family is willing for you to serve. If so, we see no reason for refusing their request. Yes, some people may misunderstand it and criticize you, but God's servants are accustomed to being misunderstood. We have never felt it necessary to ask a liberal minister or a cult leader to share in a funeral service, but we have felt it ethical to have the funeral director inform them of the family's request. These problems aren't always easy to solve, and we must be "wise as serpents and harmless as doves" (Matthew 10:16 NKJV). "Everyone should be fully convinced in their own mind" (Romans 14:5 TNIV).

A MEMBER OF THE MINISTER'S FAMILY

Most ministers will not be expected to conduct the funeral service for their life's mate or one of their children, although it has been done. An evangelist friend of ours preached at his wife's funeral, using Ezekiel 24:18 as his text, but not everybody can mourn and minister at the same time. Many ministers have triumphantly preached at the funeral of a parent, a sibling, or an in-law, but we must be certain we are up to it before we agree to serve. Perhaps it would help to have a close ministerial friend share the service "just in case." We might add that the committal service—that final good-bye—may be just as difficult as bringing the message, if not more so, and you might want to have someone else take charge. Nobody will criticize you.

If you do share in a family service, keep in mind that "family secrets" should remain in family hearts. A funeral service isn't the best place to divulge family secrets or tell funny family stories—although a certain amount of humor is acceptable at a memorial service. Also, be careful how you address unconverted family members, and don't use your pulpit privileges to intimidate them, embarrass them, or pressure them into "making a decision." If our own witness to the family has been loving and consistent, we won't have to use guilt to win the lost and reclaim the careless.

There have been occasions when a death in a minister's family has attracted the attention of the whole community. We recall a pastor's son who collapsed and died while playing a high school basketball game, and the funeral service brought many to faith in Christ. We have also seen the death of a little child open many doors of opportunity for the minister and the family as other sorrowing parents sought their help. The prophet Ezekiel "sat where they sat" (Ezekiel 3:15 KJV), and there are times when we must do the same thing and experience some of the grief and suffering that our people experience.

DEATH OF A FORMER PASTOR OF THE CHURCH

If a former pastor of your present church dies, whether active or retired, how much you can do depends on where the pastor lives and where the burial will take place. As pastor, you may not be expected to drop everything and attend the service, but perhaps some of the older members of the church are free to travel and represent the congregation. Of course, the church will send a floral tribute and/or contribute to whatever ministry or charity the family selected, and your board will send an official letter of tribute and condolence. You will also remember the family in your Sunday pastoral prayer.

If the deceased minister had been residing in the area and perhaps was still a member of the church, then your involvement will increase, and you may be asked to share in the funeral service and even to bring a message. Not everyone in the church will have the same opinion of the ministry of the deceased. Perhaps there had even been a serious break in the church's fellowship with the minister. But this is no time for exhuming the past and doing an autopsy. Let it rest. Love still covers a multitude of sins, and love "keeps no record of wrongs" (1 Peter 4:8; 1 Corinthians 13:5). The people named in Hebrews 11 all sinned and made mistakes, but there isn't a word of criticism anywhere in the chapter. Hebrews 13:7–8 instructs us to remember our spiritual leaders and what they taught us and to imitate their lives as they pointed to Christ and followed Him. Leaders change, but "Jesus Christ is the same yesterday and today and forever."

One word of caution: the home going of a former pastor sometimes motivates his family, and perhaps some zealous friends to want to set up some kind of memorial. This request must go to the board and must not be decided quickly or by people outside the congregation; otherwise the memorial may become a millstone instead of a milestone. If a memorial fund is established, then you and your leaders must pray and discuss the matter, consult with the family members, and give yourselves time to determine how the fund will be set up and administered. Your church lawyer must be involved, lest you find yourself doing a good thing in a bad way. Take time, investigate thoroughly, pray, and seek most of all to honor the Lord through the memory of His servant.

DEATH AND THE CALENDAR

Just as traffic stops for a funeral procession, so personal and family schedules are suspended and even changed when a death occurs. There is no convenient time for death, and our times must always be in His hands (Psalm 31:15). The clock and the calendar go right on, and if we know how to use it, the calendar can work for us as we plan. Use your sanctified imagination and pray for God's guidance.

THE CHRISTMAS SEASON (ADVENT) is traditionally a time of joy, which means it is an especially difficult time for families that are going through the valley. For years to come, the memory of a deceased loved one can cast a shadow over the season. However, even death can't rob us of the joy that came to earth when Jesus was born (Luke 2:8–14). That first Christmas night the Lord sent light in the midst of darkness, peace in the midst of fear, and joy and praise in the midst of the difficulties of life, and it was all because of Jesus. Isaiah wrote about people "walking in darkness . . . [and] living in the land of the shadow of death" (Isaiah 9:2), and by the time Matthew quoted the statement, the people were "sitting in darkness" because they had given up all hope (4:13–15 NASB, NKJV, NLT). But Jesus is the Light of the World (John 8:12) and brings us the light of life.

The death of a child near or during the Advent season is very painful to the family, but we must remember that innocent children were slain by Herod because of the birth of Jesus (Matthew 2:16–18). Even Rachel, one of the "mothers" of the Jewish nation, wept over her children (Jeremiah 31:15–17).

Yet we don't remember Bethlehem as a place of death (see Genesis 35:16–20) but as a place of life—for Jesus was born there! The two names of her baby speak volumes. When we live by sight, we say "son of my sorrow"; but by faith, we can say "son of my right hand." Jesus is both: He experienced sorrow and death, yet today He is at the right hand of the Father and able to help us. Yes, Bethlehem was a burial place, but Jesus transformed it into a birthplace!

NEW YEAR'S DAY   reminds us of the promise in Revelation 21:5, "I am making everything new!" Study the context and discover what these "new things" are and how "newness of life" in Christ Jesus gives us encouragement in our sorrow.

EPIPHANY (JANUARY 6)   celebrates the coming of the magi to worship Jesus (Matthew 2:1–12) and the "revelation" (epiphany) of God's glory to the Gentiles (see Luke 2:20–32). The gospel message was for the Gentiles as well as the Jews. We worship a glorified God-man in heaven, not a little child, and we have a complete Bible to guide us. The emphasis on God's glory has a healing ministry to people of faith, especially when we remind them of the future glory that belongs to every believer (Romans 8:18; Revelation 21–22).

LENTEN AND EASTER SEASON reminds us that Jesus suffered death (Good Friday) and then arose from the dead in glorious victory. Jesus willingly surrendered to death, experienced it to the full, and defeated death in His resurrection. His final statement from the cross—"Father, into your hands I commit my spirit" (Luke 23:46)—was actually a Jewish child's bedtime prayer (Psalm 31:5). It tells us that Jesus died confidently, willingly, and victoriously, and that the Father was right there with Him. The words of the angel at the empty tomb are good news for us: "He is not here; he has risen, just as he said" (Matthew 28:6). Each time we visit the grave of a loved one, we can say the same words: "He/she is not here." We don't seek the living among the dead, and we know that one day Jesus will return and the dead body won't even be there! Focus on the resurrection assurances in 1 Corinthians 15 and strengthen the hope of the sorrowing (1 Thessalonians 4:13–18).

MOTHER'S DAY AND FATHER'S DAY remind us of the "motherhood of God" and the "fatherhood of God." Motherhood? Yes! Like a mother, He loves us without measure (Isaiah 49:14–16), comforts us (Isaiah 66:13), and sings over us to quiet our hearts (Zephaniah 3:16–17). Jesus wept over those who rejected Him and would have gathered them as a hen her chicks (Matthew 23:37–39). As for fatherhood, there are many Scripture passages that can speak to the broken heart, including Psalm 103:13; Deuteronomy 1:30; Psalm 68:5; Luke 10:21–22; 1 Corinthians 1:3; James 1:17; and 1 John 3:1–2.

JUNE WEDDINGS are sometimes celebrated the same week as a funeral. In fact, we had one wedding the very evening of the day the groom's father was buried. It seemed impossible to reschedule the wedding, but the family wisely canceled the reception. We did not conduct the funeral, but the perfect funeral text would have been "Rejoice with those who rejoice; mourn with those who mourn" (Romans 12:15). Life is a "land of hills and valleys" (Deuteronomy 11:8–12), and the valleys and hills are often close to each other.

Another text would be the great "hallelujah chorus" of Revelation 19:1–9 that describes the great wedding feast of the victorious Lamb of God. First Corinthians 15:57–58 is another "hallelujah" text that is especially meaningful at the Easter season and in the spring when new life is appearing.

HARVEST SEASON AND THANKSGIVING emphasize life out of death. The seed is planted into the ground, dies, and brings forth fruit and beauty. Paul used this image in 1 Corinthians 15:20–28 and 35–49, when he wrote of "Jesus Christ the firstfruits" (v. 20; see also Leviticus 23:9–14) and the body of the believer as a seed awaiting the harvest of glory. Be sure to focus on the closing "victory verses" (vv. 57–58). Job 5:26 is a splendid verse for the funeral of a senior saint, especially if they were farmers, and see also Job 24:24.

These are only suggestions. If you are carefully cultivating your "sermonic seed plot," you should have some messages coming to maturity, and the Lord will give you guidance in adapting them to each occasion. In fact, you can ignore the calendar completely in your message, although this is difficult to do at certain seasons. The important thing is that the message fits the occasion and meets the needs of the family and friends who need comfort.

Notes

1. For help on the problem of evil in the world, see: *Don't Waste Your Sorrows,* by Paul E. Billheimer (Christian Literature Crusade, 1977); *When God Doesn't Make Sense,* by James Dobson (Tyndale, 1993); *When Heaven Is Silent,* by Ron Dunn (Thomas Nelson, 1994); *Tracks of a Fellow Struggler,* by John Claypool (Word, 1974); *Making Sense Out of Suffering,* by Peter Kreeft (Servant, 1986); *Evil and the Christian God,* by Michael Peterson (Baker, 1982); *Why? On Suffering, Guilt and God,* by A. Van de Beek (Eerdmans, 1990); *Why Us? When Bad Things Happen to Good People,* by Warren W. Wiersbe (Revell, 1984; also Chris-tian Literature Crusade edition, *When Life Falls Apart,* 2002); *Where Is God When It Hurts?* by Philip Yancey (Zondervan, 1977).

2. See also chapter 7.

Questions Pastors and Mourners Ask

PASTORS

HOW IMPORTANT TO MY PASTORAL WORK IS THE CONDUCTING OF FUNERALS?

You want to be known as a shepherd who cares. Jesus goes with us through the valley, and we should follow His loving example (Psalm 23:4). He came to "heal the brokenhearted" (Luke 4:18 KJV), and He uses His people to encourage this healing process. The pastor would certainly conduct the funeral of a high-profile church officer, but what about the lesser-known people in the congregation or a stranger? "Do not be proud, but be willing to associate with people of low position. Do not be conceited" (Romans 12:16). What Paul wrote to the slaves applies to all of us: "Serve wholeheartedly, as if you were serving the Lord, not men" (Ephesians 6:7). As we suggested earlier, try to work ahead so that the extra pressure won't set you back in your regular work. However, don't look upon a funeral as an irritating interruption, or your attitude will show. After all, Jesus was often interrupted. The interruptions are usually the ministry.

We have known churches where associate pastors were frequently requested to conduct funeral services. The senior pastor was perceived as emotionally distant from his people, an ivory-tower scholar, or a busy CEO. This is unfortunate.

If you walk with the Lord daily, spend time in the Word and with your people, and seek the help of the Holy Spirit, you will always have "a word in season," and it will be the right word. Sometimes the message we've been seeking has come to us a few hours before the funeral, but its coming was the result of mental and spiritual preparation. Keep planting and watering the seed, and the Lord will send the harvest.

Is THERE ANY BIBLICAL BASIS FOR THE SO-CALLED STAGES OF BEREAVEMENT?

As you minister to the bereaved, you will find that they do go through definable stages in accepting and dealing with grief. We're not sure you can find all of these stages in one place in the Bible, and in the order we've given, but the stages are there. Read the first chapter of the Lamentations of Jeremiah and you will find the prophet moving from tears and unrest to bitterness (1:1–4), and then from remembering (1:7) to the feeling that his grief is worse than anybody else's (1:12). Throughout that first chapter, he feels alone and senses that nobody cares (1:2, 9, 17, 21). You will find similar expressions in some of the psalms, coupled with anger, doubt, and fear.

But the five suggested stages can be of help if we use them properly. Most important, we should avoid playing "amateur psychiatrist" unless we have training and experience in counseling. It's dangerous and hurtful to be analyzing when we should be sympathizing. To press people's expressions of their feelings into a preconceived mold is neither Christian nor professional, so avoid it.

SHOULD WE THEN JUST WAIT AND LET PEOPLE WORK THROUGH THEIR GRIEF?

No, we must assist and encourage them in the healing process. Time is neutral and doesn't bring healing automatically. It's what we do with time that counts. When somebody loses a loved one, the feeling is akin to an amputation. The amputation hurts and takes time to heal, but the part removed can't be replaced.

Most people eventually make the transition successfully if given enough love and encouragement. If grieving people cut themselves off from society and sit home feeling sorry for themselves, the healing process will stop, and the person will probably become very self-centered and immature. If this stage goes on too long, professional help may be needed. It doesn't work to try to occupy them with shopping sprees, trips, and other activities, because these are only distractions that can never get to the heart of the problem. Sometimes people prolong their grieving to punish themselves for some imagined harm done to the deceased. Pastors, doctors, family members, and friends can work together to encourage healing.

I BELONG TO A FELLOWSHIP THAT IS STRONG ON EVANGELISM AND CALLING FOR IMMEDIATE SALVIFIC DECISIONS. YOU SUGGEST THAT WE "PLAY DOWN" THINGS SUCH AS INVITATIONS AND PREACHING ABOUT JUDGMENT. WHO IS RIGHT?

We have never suggested that a pastor "play down" the gospel or any truth found in the Bible, including God's judgment of sinners. The danger we're pointing out is that grieving people are very vulnerable and it's wrong to take advantage of them when they are at their weakest. Their "decision for Christ" may be very emotional but not very authentic. The pastor who said, "Preaching to lost sinners at funerals is like shooting fish in a barrel!" needed to be reminded that fishermen in the Bible used either hooks or nets and not bullets. Nobody likes to be cornered and exploited; it's unethical, unloving, and unchristian. In seeking to "win" people, we may end up losing them and deepening their prejudices against the gospel and the church.

If it's the accepted and expected thing in your area to give a strong gospel invitation at funerals, then your doing so won't alienate people, except perhaps relatives or friends who traveled from a distance. An invitation to receive Christ can be handled by some ministers with grace and skill so that they build bridges instead of walls. If the funeral service is conducted in your own church sanctuary, you have the freedom to do as you feel the Lord is leading.

Keep in mind that the major purpose for a funeral service is to minister comfort to the grieving, and that the harvest is the end of the age, not the end of the meeting. In the days following the funeral, the Lord usually gives us opportunities to minister to the family and friends of the deceased, and then we can reinforce what they heard us preach and perhaps have the joy of seeing them trust Jesus. It's possible to communicate the gospel clearly and compellingly while refraining from high-pressure tactics.

HOW CAN WE ENCOURAGE OUR CHURCH FAMILY TO ATTEND FUNERALS AND SHARE IN MINISTERING TO THE BEREAVED?

By our example and patient instruction. People are very busy these days, and life can't be shut down just because somebody has died. Most people can't afford to take off work in order to attend a funeral, but they can take time to attend the evening visitation at the funeral home. On the evening of the day of the funeral, some congregations are now hosting a reception at the church in honor of the deceased, and this gives working people opportunity to meet the family and express their sympathy. A "memory table" with photos of the deceased and other memorabilia keeps the focus on life and not on death. Some families prepare a video or DVD reviewing the life of the deceased.

But we need to remind our people that Christians have an obligation to "mourn with those who mourn" (Romans 12:15). If there are care groups in your church, this is a fine opportunity for them to practice their faith and reveal that they are maturing in the Lord. Find out who the people are in the congregation who have a gift of helps and mercy, and put them to work. How we thank the Lord for the men and women who sacrifice to prepare postfuneral lunches and organize people to take meals to homes! As we serve the Lord's people, we serve the Lord.

Sometimes transportation to the funeral is the problem, so appoint people to supervise this aspect of ministry. This is especially important for the elderly. In your pulpit ministry, remind your people that Christians belong to each other and need each other, and that personal ministry in times of sorrow is vitally important. On the Sunday following a funeral, remember to thank publicly the people who served in special ways. (You don't have to name them.) It's also important to have people keep contact with the bereaved in the weeks that follow.

In some urban areas, the actual funeral service is held at the funeral home after the visitation, a practice more convenient for both the family and the guests. The graveside service is held the next morning for family and those they invite to join them. This can complicate the pastor's schedule a bit, but we still are available and do our best for the Lord.

AS PASTORS, WE "PERFORM WEDDINGS," BUT WHAT'S THE RIGHT VERB FOR WHAT WE DO AT FUNERALS?

The verb is probably *conduct*. We don't like to hear pastors say, "I have to do a funeral." It sounds so impersonally routine and mechanical. And never imitate the young pastor who called to a friend, "I have to go downtown and read over a stiff!" Anyone who would describe a Christian funeral as "reading over a stiff" should be drummed out of the ministry.

I REALLY CAN'T STAND THE "CANNED MUSIC" THEY PLAY IN SOME FUNERAL HOMES. WHAT CAN BE DONE ABOUT IT?

If that's what the family selected, you can't do very much about it. People need to be reminded that a funeral is a person's "last will and testimony," and that includes the music. But if the family requests a soloist, this means securing a pianist or organist or providing equipment for playing tracks. Having a singer and accompanist adds to the funeral expenses, although some churches have wonderful people who will provide these services as a ministry and expect nothing in return. However, as an expression of thanks, it is proper for the family to give an honorarium to those who serve.

It's tragic but true that most people are accustomed to "canned music" in their vehicles, in elevators, at the dentist's office, and in the supermarkets. Don't get too critical. Accept what is planned, and make sure your part in the service isn't "canned."

ARE PEOPLE REALLY LISTENING AT FUNERALS?

Yes and no. Emotions can overwhelm people and become very distracting. We can encourage engaged attention if we, in the service, get people's names right and give evidence by our words that we knew the deceased person. Alas, many people are there just to fulfill the "funeral ritual," but we never know how the Lord may speak to them through the occasion and the message. It may take years even for a clear statement of truth to take root in the heart and bear fruit, and God promises that His Word will always accomplish His will (Isaiah 55:8–11; Galatians 6:9).

WHAT KIND OF FUNERAL RECORDS MUST I KEEP?

Check with the clerk of the circuit court or with an experienced local pastor. The church is supposed to keep permanent records of deaths and funerals, and you can secure a personal record book for both funerals and weddings. You will also want to keep a record of the funeral messages you gave, if only to keep from repeating yourself. Both you and the church clerk should have accurate records so that if God calls you elsewhere, you won't walk off with the records. Some funeral directors give the pastor an official record of the funeral, and this can be copied for you and the original placed in the church files.

Keep your notes from interviews with family members, because you may be asked to conduct a service for the spouse or another relative later on. We have been greatly helped by referring to our records of the previous service and the obituary. It helps to keep family relationships accurate, and if the family wants something repeated from the previous service, you know what it was and who did it.

WHAT'S THE SIGNIFICANCE OF OUR WALKING BEFORE THE CASKET AS WE ENTER OR LEAVE THE CHURCH, OR STANDING AT THE HEAD OF THE CASKET AT THE GRAVESIDE SERVICE?

In some Christian communions, the presiding minister enters the church or chapel before the casket with a censer and diffuses incense. Churches that don't include incense in their liturgy feel that the presiding minister should lead the way since the minister is the shepherd of the flock. If several ministers are involved in the funeral service, the local pastor can go before the casket and the others enter from the side and go to the platform. Just keep it simple and listen to the funeral director.

We're not sure that standing at the head of the casket at the graveside is necessarily a tradition anymore, but it's still a good custom. The minister must stand somewhere, and at the head seems the logical place. We've shared in committal services where other participants stood beside the casket toward the center, and nobody was upset. Most important is that the gathered family and friends be able to hear what is said and know when they are supposed to participate in group liturgy (prayer, the Lord's Prayer, a song).

WHAT'S THE BEST WAY TO BEGIN A FUNERAL SERVICE IN A FUNERAL HOME? PEOPLE ARE OFTEN TALKING, MOVING AROUND THE CHAPEL, OR CLUSTERED AT THE CASKET, AND I NEED TO GET THEIR ATTENTION AND ORGANIZE THEM INTO A CONGREGATION.

The funeral director is a great help here. A minute or two before the time announced for the service, he or she walks with an assistant up to the front, closes the casket, and one of them turns on the light at the lectern. They wait quietly for a moment and then retire. The signal has been given that the service is about to begin. You walk up to the casket even if it is closed, and pause with bowed head and pray for God's help, and then go to the lectern. Give the stragglers time to sit down and get settled, and then begin by quoting or reading Scripture. We have often opened with 1 John 3:1–2 and then 1 Peter 1:3–5. Pause and then offer a brief but heartfelt invocation.

If you are meeting in the church sanctuary or a chapel in the church edifice, the closing of the casket signals the entrance of the minister to the pulpit. If the organ has been playing quietly, it is now time for the organist to increase the volume enough to let the congregation know the service has begun. When the funeral is on church premises, we like to open with the Scripture quotations, an invocation, and then a hymn. This gives latecomers an opportunity to find their places.

Many people rarely attend funerals and don't understand the protocol, so don't be too hard on them. Once you have their attention, be sure to preach your best so you don't lose that attention.

WHAT SHOULD WE DO WITH BABIES AT FUNERAL SERVICES?

Endure them and love them. Sometimes the mother has to bring the baby because there's nobody available to care for the child at home. Let's at least be grateful that she cares enough for the deceased to go to all that trouble to be present. The wise funeral director seats a mother and child near the back and on the aisle in case there must be a hasty exit. If the service is at the church, perhaps you can recruit qualified nursery workers to tend the children during the service. We recall a secretary at a funeral home who left her desk to care for a fussy child and thus helped the mother, the family, and the pastor. May her tribe increase!

SHOULD THE MEN WEAR THEIR HATS AT THE GRAVESIDE SERVICE?

Yes, if the weather is frigid and the men are liable to catch colds. This includes the pallbearers and the ministers. Take your cue from the funeral director and feel free to announce the decision. As we have said before, one of the best ways to honor the dead is to take care of the living. When the Prince of Preachers, Charles Haddon Spurgeon, was buried in Highgate Cemetery, London, the participants kept their hats on.

The cemetery staff usually erects a marquee at the gravesite to provide shelter from the wind and cold, and many cemeteries now have small chapels where the committal service may be held. After the guests depart, the casket is taken to the gravesite and placed into the vault and the grave covered. We prefer to be at the gravesite for the committal service, but in inclement weather, the chapel is a welcome refuge.

If the weather is bad, keep the service brief.

HOW LONG SHOULD THE FAMILY REMAIN AT THE GRAVESIDE FOLLOWING THE COMMITTAL SERVICE?

As long as it takes them to thank people and say good-bye. If there's a meal to be served at the church, lingering too long can make it difficult for the servers. Some family members may need a few extra minutes for that final farewell, and there is also the tradition of giving each family member a flower from the casket spray. Some people want to remain and see the casket lowered into the vault and the grave filled in, but a member of the funeral home staff usually remains behind to witness this event.

We must bear in mind that many cemeteries have multiple interments each day, and their staff is under pressure to get their work done on time. However, we should let the funeral director handle these matters, since he works with these staff people regularly and they know him.

I'VE HEARD HORROR STORIES ABOUT PREPLANNED FUNERALS AND THE ABUSE OF FUNDS BY FUNERAL DIRECTORS, AS WELL AS PRESSURE TACTICS IN SELLING CASKETS.

Every profession has its shysters, so don't condemn all funeral directors because of what a few may have done. About 25 percent of the funerals conducted in the United States are under a prepaid or pre-need plan. It's wise to choose a mortician who belongs to one of their industry's professional organizations, such as the National Funeral Directors Association or Selected Independent Funeral Homes. The home should also belong to the local Chamber of Commerce and the Better Business Bureau. Each of these organizations has a code of ethics that requires members to be honest and efficient in the services they render. In most communities and neighborhoods, if a funeral director seems to be engaging in shady dealings, the word soon gets out and people know about it. You can always contact the Better Business Bureau to check a funeral home's reputation.

In most states, prepaid or pre-need plans are controlled by law, the money is placed in escrow and is protected, and the funeral home contracted with must fulfill the contract, even if the home is under different management since the agreement was signed. *If you are asked for a down payment before they provide you with all the information needed, look for another funeral director.* It's also important to know if there's a penalty for dropping the plan or changing it. Do some shopping around and read the fine print. Not all pre-need plans are the same.

The prepaid funeral relieves the survivors of having to make difficult decisions at a time when it's not easy to know what the deceased had in mind. But it is a business deal and as such deserves to be examined carefully. Be sure that the products and services were exactly what the funeral director promised in the contract. However, even if there is a pre-need agreement, family members may still have to select the casket and make minor decisions not specified in the contract.

You can go online and locate a number of funeral directors' associations that provide free information as well as their code of ethics. The

AARP has information on various aspects of the funeral industry, and so does the Funeral Service Consumer Assistance Program. Check their Web sites.

WHAT ABOUT PEOPLE PLACING LETTERS, TOYS, AND OTHER MEMORABILIA INTO THE CASKET?

This can be evidence of a close relationship between the person and the deceased, and if this helps a grieving person, we see no serious problem. However, it's best that the family members in charge be contacted first to give their approval, or the casket may get cluttered. The deceased doesn't know the items are there, and you don't want to overdo it. A child's favorite toy in the casket can be meaningful to the loved ones, but perhaps the rest of the toy box ought to be donated to a church nursery or a day care center.

WHAT'S THE BEST WAY TO MAKE USE OF THE FLORAL TRIBUTES THAT PEOPLE SEND? SOME OF THEM ARE TAKEN TO THE CEMETERY, BUT MANY REMAIN BACK AT THE FUNERAL HOME.

Many people no longer send floral tributes but instead make contributions to the deceased person's local church or favorite charity. While it's lovely to have beautiful flowers around the casket, the tradition can be overdone.

If the family wants the church to have flowers for the next Sunday's services, the chosen displays should be set aside and given to somebody who can "repackage" them into lovely bouquets. People can spot a funeral floral display a mile away. If you take flowers to shut-ins or to elderly people in retirement homes, first put them into cheery arrangements.

In lieu of sending flowers, friends may use the cards and envelopes provided by the funeral home for financial gifts to be sent to ministries or charities chosen by the family. People may send gifts to their own favorite ministries, and the family would accept this.

WHAT ABOUT HUMOR AT A FUNERAL OR MEMORIAL SERVICE?

Suitable humor is permissible at the memorial service as people remember the life of the deceased, for funny things do happen to people. A bit of wit might fit into a funeral message, but we ministers must not become stand-up comedians, especially at funerals. But please don't introduce laughter at the graveside burial service, because that final good-bye is serious. God's people aren't afraid of healthy laughter; in fact, doctors tell us that ten minutes of laughter can relieve us of two hours of stress. "A cheerful heart is good medicine" (Proverbs 17:22), but even the best medicine could do harm unless taken in the right amount and at the right time. The discerning shepherd will know when humor will be received as medicine and when it will add to the pain.

DOES ANYBODY HAVE THE RIGHT TO OVERRIDE THE DESIRES OF THE DECEASED, OR MUST THE FAMILY OBEY THEIR EVERY WHIM?

Some people leave behind a description of what they want at their funeral or memorial service, and the family should follow these requests as much as possible. Perhaps a husband and wife have even talked over their plans with each other and with their children. (A written document is better. We all have selective memories.) But sometimes people's hearts run ahead of their brains, and they ask for silly things that would only mar the service and send people home with bad memories of a good person.

As ministers of the gospel, we don't have the right to interfere with the desires of the deceased or the decisions of the family, unless somebody with authority asks for our opinion or unless the funeral is to be held on church premises. A blind man who died had requested that the trustees of the church allow his guide dog to be present, and this was no problem, for the dog would have been there if the man had still been alive. But this one logical concession doesn't mean that Mrs. Smith's pet parrot or little Susie's pet gerbil should also attend the funeral. Service animals are protected by law and may go places where pets in general are prohibited.

Sometimes feelings of guilt take control and family members try to atone for their own "sins against the deceased"—imagined or real—by insisting on absolute conformity to the loved one's desires. It's then that the patient funeral director and the pastor must work together to bring light and love into the situation and suggest acceptable alternatives. Pets aren't allowed in the church or funeral home chapel, but there's no reason why photos of pets can't be on display. We think that the spouse and other surviving family members have the right to eliminate from the funeral service anything that would compromise the gospel or trivialize the seriousness of the occasion or the reputation or witness of the deceased. Everybody in the family may not agree, but somebody has to make a decision. As to how much input you can give, it all depends on the situation and the dynamics of the family (James 1:5).

HOW CAN WE DEFUSE A "POWER STRUGGLE" IN A BLENDED FAMILY?

We may not be able to. In fact, if we aren't careful, we may make it worse. All of us like to see family members cooperate in love, but some people aren't capable of controlling their desires and coping with death at the same time, and some people are just immature. They argue about trivial matters, or they lay down ultimatums that verge on declarations of war. A week later they wish they had kept quiet, but they may not admit it or apologize. Try to identify the family members who seem to have a balanced perspective, and quietly encourage them to use their influence toward a win-win compromise and not a win-lose conquest.

However, be alert; once the service begins, anything can happen. We recall a funeral service at which the deceased man's first wife marched majestically up the aisle and took a front-row seat, refusing to respect the widow's feelings or privileges. To interfere would have given the ex-wife the attention she was seeking and perhaps have ruined the whole service, so we all ignored the woman and let her make a fool out of herself.

AFTER CONDUCTING THE FUNERAL OF SOMEONE NOT CONNECTED WITH OUR CHURCH, HOW CAN I ESTABLISH ONGOING CONTACT WITH THE FAMILY AND FRIENDS WITHOUT APPEARING TO BE "RECRUITING" THEM FOR OUR CHURCH?

Postfuneral ministry is very important and you never know how the Lord may work in hearts. If the family chose you to conduct the service, then they must have confidence in you and probably won't be suspicious if you stay in contact. If they gave you an honorarium for your services, you must write them a thank-you note, and in it you can say you would like to visit them again. If the funeral director asked for your help at the funeral, then perhaps he can build some bridges for you. Are there people in your church who know the family? Then let them help pave the way. In that first visit, make it clear that your concern is to assist them and not enlist them. If nothing seems to be developing, step aside for a time, and when the first anniversary of the person's death comes around, drop the widow, widower, or family a note and pray for the Lord to open doors and hearts. We have seen God do wonderful things in postfuneral contacts, so don't be so timid you miss the opportunities God gives you. "Wise as serpents, harmless as doves."

I HAVE A MINISTER FRIEND WHO CONDUCTS SERVICES FOR DEAD PETS, USUALLY DOGS OR CATS. IS THIS REALLY ONE OF MY MINISTRIES AS A PASTOR?

Pick the right Sunday and you can drive to certain churches where the ministers will bless you and your car, and if your dog and cat are along, give them a blessing too. There are more pet cats in the United States than there are pet dogs, although there are 50 to 60 million pet dogs. If you have ever visited a "pet supermarket," you know that the care and feeding of animals is big business. Eventually all these pets will die, and then what?

But before we answer the question, let's see what Scripture says about animal life.

There's no evidence in Scripture that animals have souls, that they are accountable to God for their actions and therefore will be judged, or that they will be resurrected and participate in the future hope. Animals were created for the good of mankind (Genesis 9:3), and God cares for them (Psalm 104:16-17, 20–30) and wants us to treat them with kindness (Exodus 23:12; Leviticus 25:1–17; Deuteronomy 25:4; Proverbs 12:10). When Noah and his family emerged from the ark, God made a covenant with them and also with the animals that had been preserved in the ark (Genesis 9:8–17). The four faces of the cherubim represent God's creatures: the man, the ox (domesticated animals), the lion (wild animals), and the eagle (birds). (See Ezekiel 1:1–14 and Revelation 4:6–8.) In its own way, animal creation praises the Lord and depends on Him for life and sustenance (Psalms 148:7–12; 147:9). Note in Jonah 4:11 God's concern for young children and helpless animals. Jesus remarked about

God's care for the birds (Matthew 6:25–27; 10:29–31) and God's approval of those who care for their farm animals (Luke 14:1–6).

But is there any future for animals that have died, wild or domesticated? Some believe that Romans 8:18–25 affirms a future for our pets since animals are a part of God's expectant creation. But when Paul says "the whole creation," does he mean every living thing that has ever existed—every insect, fish, animal, bird, and human? We don't think so, because in verses 22–23, he differentiates between the groaning of "all creation" and the groaning of Christian believers. This implies that in the future kingdom, animal life will not be treated the same way as human life. Heaven is not "earth with a face-lift." Heaven is so wonderful that John ran out of metaphors to describe it!

Now, to answer the question.

As servants of the Lord, we want to meet the needs of our people. There's no denying that pets are loved and wanted, and when they die, their owners grieve and miss them. That being the case, we must in compassion minister to those who hurt. *But to encourage grief over the death of a pet as you would over the death of a son or daughter, parent, or spouse is to make the pet an idol that, alive or dead, so controls the owners that they have their priorities all confused.* Yes, let's minister to the needs of the owners in their loss, but no, let's not treat animals, dead or alive, like people. If we start treating like people the animals we love, it's but a short step to treating like animals the people we ought to love.

Let's imagine that we were called to visit the Abbott home where the pet dog Fuzzy had died from being struck by a car. On arriving, we would first of all sincerely express our sympathy, because the death of a pet is painful, especially for the children in the family. Second, we would read some of the verses that reveal God's special interest in and care for animals, emphasizing that they are a part of God's great creation. Third, we would ask, "Has anybody in the family been abusive or cruel to Fuzzy? Don't admit it openly, but as we all bow to pray, you ask God to forgive you." Finally, we would pray for the whole family, asking the Lord to give them healing and comfort, to forgive any abuses and reward faithful care. *This helps to prepare the way for any new pets that may enter the family.* We would then leave the family to dispose of the remains as they see fit.

We see no reason for a special committal service that requires the services of a pastor. Our ministry is primarily to the grieving family, especially the children. However, most metropolitan areas now have pet funeral homes, crematories, and cemeteries to serve those who want special disposal of their dead pets, including caskets and grave markers with epitaphs. There is an International Association of Pet Cemeteries (IAPC) serving the pet funeral industry. "All Pets Go to Heaven" is the name of a pet funeral home in New York, and in Connecticut there is an "Eternal Love Pet Cemetery." In Virginia you find "Noah's Ark Pet Cemetery," and Texas boasts "Paws in Heaven" pet cemetery.

Some older couples treat their pets like members of the family—maybe better!—and are deeply hurt by the death of a longtime pet. Again, we respond not to the death of the animal but to the pain of the owners. When people have lived with a pet for many years, there's an attachment that may seem trivial to some but is very important to the owners. People who have never had a long, satisfying relationship with a pet often become critical, cynical, and sarcastic and can't understand why anybody would shed tears over a dead animal. The minister's task is to help the owners get some perspective on the situation and transition into the next stage in life, be it no pet at all or a pet replacement.

Again, this kind of ministry isn't something the pastor makes his top priority; he wouldn't interrupt a wedding ceremony to make a house call on a dying pet. But we must keep sensitive to the hurts of our people, especially children and the elderly, and seek to help people mature in the faith and discover the healing grace of God. We don't make unbiblical promises that pets will be in heaven, but we do promise that when we get to heaven, there will be no more tears, and we'll understand better why things happened as they did.

HOW DO WE RESPOND TO FAMILIES THAT WANT TO TELL THE CHURCH HOW MEMORIAL FUNDS SHOULD BE USED?

We've encountered family members who were insistent about "running things" to the point of assuming authority that they did not have in the church. If people contributed funds to the church in memory of the deceased, and received an official receipt, then the money belongs to the church and not the donors or the family. But even if they gave by using the special envelopes at the funeral home, and the funeral director gave the money to the family member nearest to the deceased, they cannot tell the church how to use it. Some churches have a "living remembrance fund" into which all memorial gifts are placed, and from this fund they finance specific ministries approved by the church. This is one way to prevent competition and political maneuvering. Yes, church members do such things, especially if they are hurting from grief or want to immortalize their dead loved one.

Once the funds are given to the church, the church officers make the decision after conferring with the loved ones. Your church trustees will want to chat with your church attorney about this whole matter.

Every church should have a policy for handling memorial funds, and this policy must be made known to the members. Memorial funds should be used to benefit the entire church family and not just a chosen few, and they should be used for something that will endure. The memorial committee will have to pray, investigate needs, and confer with the family. It's wise to have a Book of Remembrance that records the names of the deceased and how the memorial funds were used, but not the amount of the funds or the names of the donors.

How do we help family members answer children's questions asked at the visitation, at the funeral, or at home after the funeral?

We need patience and wisdom. To tell children to "hush" or to give them a meaningless generic answer is to show disrespect and create even greater problems. Keep three principles in mind: (1) show love and respect; (2) try to discern "the question behind the question"; and (3) give a reasonable answer appropriate to the child's level of maturity and understanding.

Consider this scenario. At the visitation, five-year-old Randy stood by his grandfather's casket for a long time, looking as if he were pondering some great question. Finally he asked his mother, "Where are his feet?" Wisely, the mother had the funeral director open the closed part of the casket and show Randy that Grandpa was "all there," and the boy was satisfied. But often the questions are much more difficult. "If Jesus loves us, why did He take my mother away?" "If Grandpa's in heaven, why are we making all this fuss about his body?" "Am I to blame for what happened to Uncle Joe?" Imagined guilt can be a real problem with some children.

We must never teach children something that has to be untaught when they get older. We must also not give the impression that every question they can ask has a good answer, because there are some questions nobody can answer. As we have said before in these pages, we live by promises and not by explanations, and children can begin to understand this important principle.

The child who asks no questions may have greater burdens than the one who has no end of questions. Parents must take time to ask, "Is there anything about this that puzzles you?" Jesus tenderly taught His disciples *as they were able to receive the truth* (John 13:7; 16:12; Mark 4:33), and this is a good policy for us to follow.

One word of caution: if we tell children that the deceased person "is only sleeping," they may confuse death and sleep and be afraid to go to bed at night. Yes, "sleep" is a good biblical image for death (the body sleeps), but not all children can separate the metaphorical from the actual.

MOURNERS

I HEARD A CLERGYMAN SAY THAT CHILDREN WHO DIE BECOME ANGELS. IS THIS TRUE?

No, it isn't true. God created the angels before He created the worlds, and there is no evidence that He will create any more. The good angels are confirmed in their holiness and the fallen angels in their wickedness, and the fallen angels will be judged and punished in the pit. Good angels serve believers, "those who will inherit salvation" (Hebrews 1:14).

The idea that people in heaven become angels comes from a misunderstanding of Matthew 22:30. When believers go to heaven, the human relationships of earth no longer remain. Angels have neither fathers nor mothers, nor do angels marry. People on earth marry because people die, and we must perpetuate the race. In heaven, nobody dies, so marriage is unnecessary. One day we who belong to Christ will be like Him (1 John 3:1–2), *and this is a position much higher than that of angels!*

WILL OUR DECEASED CHILD REMAIN A CHILD IN HEAVEN?

The Bible doesn't give us a great deal of detailed information about the intermediate state between death and resurrection, but since heaven is a place of perfection, we would answer the question with "No." We believe that babies and little children mature in heaven and will be recognized as adults by those who knew them. How God will do this isn't revealed in Scripture.

DO OUR LOVED ONES IN HEAVEN KNOW WHAT WE'RE SAYING AND DOING HERE ON EARTH?

There is no clear biblical evidence that they do. Luke 15:7 and 10 teach that the angels in heaven rejoice when a sinner on earth is converted, and we assume that this good news would be passed along to their loved ones and friends in heaven. The martyrs in heaven knew that their murderers on earth had not yet been punished (Revelation 6:9–11), but this is a very special group of people. The "cloud of witnesses" of Hebrews 12:1 refers to the faithful saints in chapter 11 who witness to us by the record of their faith given in the Bible. It's not that they watch us but that we read about them in Scripture and witness their faith. We know that the Lord witnesses our lives, and this ought to encourage us in times of trial and temptation.

WILL WE RECOGNIZE ONE ANOTHER IN HEAVEN, INCLUDING PEOPLE WE HAVE NEVER MET?

Yes, according to 1 Corinthians 13:12. As one Bible teacher expressed it, "We certainly aren't going to be more stupid in heaven than we are here on earth." Peter, James, and John recognized Moses and Elijah on the Mount of Transfiguration, yet they had never met them (Matthew 17:1–4). Best of all, there will be nothing sinful to interfere with perfect communication, knowledge, and love.

WHEN I VISIT THE GRAVE, IS IT OKAY TO TALK TO MY LOVED ONE?

If you do, please realize that you are not communicating with your loved one at all. Make-believe leads to deeper problems and keeps us from facing reality and dealing honestly with life. It would be better to speak to the Lord and pour out your heart to Him. Or, ask a friend to accompany you to the cemetery, and the both of you chat informally about the deceased person, perhaps even laughing a bit, and then spend time in thanksgiving and prayer. What lies in the grave is not your loved one but only the body he or she lived in when alive on earth. Absent from the body means to be present with the Lord (2 Corinthians 5:1–10).

I DIDN'T FOLLOW MY HUSBAND'S WISHES EXACTLY FOR HIS FUNERAL AND BURIAL, AND NOW I FEEL GUILTY. WHAT SHOULD I DO?

Even the state funerals of important people don't always follow the wishes of the deceased, simply because circumstances change and unforeseen difficulties arise. One of the marks of maturity is the realization that the past is the past and cannot be changed, but if we live in the past and become obsessed with it, the past can change the present, and this will alter the future. What you have done won't upset some great plan God has for you; nor will it affect your husband's joy in heaven. It isn't unusual for grieving people to have feelings of guilt, but we must not allow these feelings to become obsessions. Give them to the Lord and get busy serving others. By faith, patience, and the normal activities of life, you will in time overcome these guilt feelings and regain your perspective.

I FEEL LIKE I WILL NEVER AGAIN WANT TO ATTEND A FUNERAL.

Our feelings change, so give yourself time. Other sorrowing people attended your loved one's funeral and helped to share your grief, so why shouldn't you help to share their sorrow? In fact, weeping with others is one of the best ways to heal a broken heart. People know what you're going through, and they pray for you, and you should pray for them. A joy shared doubles the joy; a grief shared halves the grief. If you pamper yourself, you can never mature in a balanced way and receive all that the Lord has for you. It may not seem like it now, but you will emerge from this tunnel and see the light again. The Lord can heal a broken heart if we give Him all the pieces.

HOW SHOULD I ACT WHEN I GO BACK TO CHURCH THE FIRST
TIME WITHOUT MY SPOUSE?

Act like a person who has been through the valley with Jesus and come
out with peace and victory. Be yourself—your best self—and seek to be a
blessing to others. Some of the people who speak to you may unwittingly
say the wrong thing, but just smile and be kind to them. The fellowship of
friends in the local church is one of the best sources of healing, so don't
isolate yourself. It takes time for new widows and widowers to fit into their
new roles, but it can be done—and it has been done! The Lord will open
new doors of fellowship and ministry for you, so let Him lead a day at a
time. The more you continue to attend worship, the more opportunity
others will have to get to know you in your changed situation and the
easier it will be for you to adjust.

I FIND THAT I DON'T WANT TO CHANGE ANYTHING AT HOME,
LEST I SEEM TO BE ERASING THE MEMORY OF MY DECEASED
SPOUSE.

One of the difficult stages of recovery is making changes in the home
without seeming to insult or destroy the memories of the past. Unless
you want to live in a museum, you must make some changes, but don't
tackle them too soon, all at once, or alone. The day will dawn when your
heart will say, "Well, now is the time!" If no understanding family
member can assist you, ask a couple of your church friends to help you
sort out clothing and other items and find places to put them to use.
Some things, of course, will never be given up because they are too precious to you. After you've conquered the closets and the dressers and
gotten over that ordeal, you may want to rearrange some furniture or
even start thinking about a bit of redecorating—or downsizing. Drastic?
Not if you're ready for it. Just don't move too quickly, and don't pull up
the roots that have taken so long to nurture.

Talk things over with the Lord, your family, and your pastor and
close friends, and follow David's counsel in Psalm 32:9, "Do not be like
the horse or mule. . . ." The horse impulsively rushes ahead, the mule
stubbornly refuses to move at all, and both suffer for their lack of bal-
ance. There is "a time to keep and a time to throw away" (Ecclesiasties

3:6), and blessed are those who understand the times. As much as we may want to preserve the past, we can't do it. We must courageously live in the present and anticipate the future. This means facing new challenges, enjoying new evidences of God's grace, and discovering new opportunities for serving others. "Jesus Christ is the same yesterday [cherish the blessings of the past] and today [walk with Him each day] and forever [trust Him for your future]" (Hebrews 13:8). The best is yet to come!

An Anthology
of Resources

Our two greatest resources for ministry are the Word of God and our walk with God as we serve Him and His people. If we follow Him faithfully, the Lord will teach us and prepare us for what He has prepared for us, and we will be ready for the many demands of ministry, including funerals. But the wise shepherd also seeks to learn from the experiences of others, and this is where books come in.

The items in this anthology are but samples of what's available, and some of these books are listed in our bibliography. The minister with a "homiletical mind-set" and a pastor's heart will immediately recognize useful material no matter where it appears and will add it to his notebook or file. So-called secular books often contain statements or historical accounts that express truths that can help us better share God's Word with others. It's well been said that "all truth is God's truth," and we may learn some great truths from writers whom we might classify as enemies of the faith.

We suggest that all who want to minister effectively to the bereaved take time to read the following literature and learn from it. Some of these you may have read during your own academic journey, but now that you are older, perhaps you ought to read them again. As you read, ask yourself, "What is the author's view of life? of death? of a future hope? of the gospel of Jesus Christ? How can this help me in my ministry to the sorrowing?"

POETRY

"Threnody" BY RALPH WALDO EMERSON
(written after the death of his little son)

"Elegy Written in a Country Churchyard" BY THOMAS GREY
(an anonymous death)

"Thanatopsis" BY WILLIAM CULLEN BRYANT
(a young man's view of death)

"In Memoriam" BY ALFRED LORD TENNYSON
(honoring a friend who died)

Spoon River Anthology BY EDGAR LEE MASTERS

PLAYS AND NOVELS

"Our Town" BY THORNTON WILDER

"Death of a Salesman" BY ARTHUR MILLER

The Death of Ivan Ilych BY LEO TOLSTOY

BIOGRAPHY AND AUTOBIOGRAPHY

Death Be Not Proud BY JOHN GUNTHER (on the death of his son)

A Grief Observed BY C. S. LEWIS (on the death of his wife)

Lament for a Son BY NICHOLAS WOOTERSTORFF

The Light That Never Dies BY WILLIAM HENDRICKS

Of course, this list is not exhaustive, but it will at least get you started. Visit your local library and share your interests with the librarian, and you will locate other titles. It does us good to read what various people, believers and unbelievers, have to say about death and the afterlife.

Another source of spiritual nourishment for the sorrowing is the church hymnal, which, next to the Bible, is a treasury of truth gathered from the witness of the church throughout the ages. Here are but a few titles that can help prepare your own heart to minister and, if sung or read at a service, can help to bring comfort to others.

"Peace, Perfect Peace" BY E. H. BICKERSTETH

"Be Still, My Soul" BY KATHARINA VON SCHLEGEL

"Face to Face" BY CARRIE E. BRECK

"Day By Day" BY LINA SANDELL

"Saved By Grace" BY FANNY J. CROSBY

"For All the Saints" BY WILLIAM W. HOW

"Come, Christians Join to Sing" BY CHRISTIAN H. BATEMAN

"Guide Me, O Thou Great Jehovah" BY WILLIAM WILLIAMS

"Jesus Lives and So Shall I" BY CHRISTIAN F. GELLERT

"There Is a Land of Pure Delight" BY ISAAC WATTS

"Ten Thousand Times Ten Thousand" BY HENRY ALFORD

Page through a good hymnal—not just a "Christian songbook"—and you will find many more fine selections. If you can find a copy of *Sacred Songs and Solos,* compiled by Ira Sankey, you will have a neglected treasury of lyrics that still speak to the hearts of God's people. It's time we imitated Isaac and "dug again the old wells" to discover how satisfying the living water really is (Genesis 26).

The selections in this brief anthology may prime your pump and help get you started on a message, and some of them you may want to quote in your message. However, not everybody in the congregation can identify C. S. Lewis, Somerset Maugham, or Phillips Brooks, so a sentence or two of explanation will help. Some of these selections are purely secular and should be used with care.

FROM JEREMY TAYLOR (1613–1667)

His book *The Rule and Exercises of Holy Dying* was published in 1651 and was very popular in his day, but what he wrote is quite contemporary.

Try to locate a copy, but be careful that it's not a "digest." These quotations are from an edition published in 1864 by Little, Brown in Boston. It's an excellent manual to guide ministers in preparing people for death.

> It is a great art to die well. (p. 1x)
>
> All that a sick and dying man can do is but to exercise those virtues which he before acquired, and to perfect that repentance which was begun more early. (p. 1x)
>
> He that would die well must always look for death, every day knocking at the gates of the grave. . . . (p. 52)
>
> He that desires to die well must all the days of his life lay up against the day of death [*a pious life*]. (p. 54)
>
> He that desires to die well and happily, above all things must be careful that he do not live a soft, a delicate and a voluptuous life, but a life severe, holy, and under the discipline of the cross. [James 4:9; Amos 6:1]
>
> He that will die well and happily must dress his soul by a diligent and frequent scrutiny: he must perfectly understand and watch the state of his soul; he must set his house in order before he be fit to die. (p. 68)
>
> In sickness the soul begins to dress herself for immortality. (p. 115)

SOME GENERAL OBSERVATIONS

I'm not afraid to die. I just don't want to be there when it happens.
WOODY ALLEN

I don't want to achieve immortality through my work. I want to achieve immortality through not dying.
WOODY ALLEN

Life is pleasant. Death is peaceful. It's the transition that's troublesome.

ISAAC ASIMOV

He [Sigmund Freud] was haunted by death anxiety all his life and admitted that not a day went by that he did not think about it.

ERNEST BECKER, *Denial of Death,* p. 102

Dying is a very dull, dreary affair. And my advice to you [his nephew] is to have nothing whatever to do with it.

SOMERSET MAUGHAM, shortly before death

As soon as we to be begun / We did begin to be undone.

OLD ENGLISH SAYING

Here I lie by the chancel door.
They put me here because I'm poor.
The further in, the more you pay.
But here I lie as snug as they.

EPITAPH IN A CHURCH IN DEVON, ENGLAND

It matters not how a man dies, but how he lives.

SAMUEL JOHNSON

Fear not that life shall come to an end, but rather fear that it shall never have a beginning.

JOHN HENRY NEWMAN

We are but tenants, and . . . shortly the great Landlord will give us notice that our lease has expired.

FROM THE INSCRIPTION ON JOSEPH
JEFFERSON'S MONUMENT,
Cape Cod, MA

Death is but a passage. It is not a house, it is only a vestibule.

ALEXANDER MACLAREN

Death is not a state but a step, not a chamber but a passage; not an abiding-place but a bridge across a gulf.

F. B. MEYER

Death is the great adventure, beside which moon landings and space trips pale into insignificance.

JOSEPH BAYLY

Life is a constant sunrise, which death cannot interrupt, any more than the night can swallow up the sun. "God is not the God of the dead, but of the living, for all live unto him."

GEORGE MACDONALD

All mankind is of one Author, and is one volume; when one man dies, one chapter is not torn out of the book, but translated into a better language; and every chapter must be so translated. God employs several translators. Some pieces are translated by age, some by sickness, some by war, some by justice. But God's hand is in every translation, and His hand shall bind up all our scattered leaves again for that Library where every book shall lie open to one another.

JOHN DONNE

No man is an island, entire of itself. Every man is a piece of the continent, a part of the main. If a clod be washed away by the sea, Europe is the less, as if a promontory were, as well as if a manor of thy friends or of thine own were. Any man's death diminishes me, because I am involved in mankind. And therefore never send to know for whom the bell tolls. It tolls for thee.

JOHN DONNE

EARLY DEATH

Let us get rid of such old wives' tales as the one that tells us it is tragic to die before one's time. What "time" is that, I would like to know? Nature is the one who has granted us the loan of our lives, without setting any schedule for repayment. What has one to complain of if she calls in the loan when she will?

CICERO

The philosopher's whole life is a preparation for death.

CICERO

When your parent dies you have lost your past. But when your child dies, you have lost your future.

ELLIOT LUBY

For the tragedy of early death is not its suffering; it is the blighted promise and the hope that is never crowned. . . . Wherever death is there you have mystery. But in the death of the young the mystery is doubled.

GEORGE H. MORRISON

What shall I think when I am called to die?
Shall I not find too soon my life has ended
The years, too quickly, have hastened by
With so little done of all that I intended.
There were so many things I'd meant to try,
So many contests I'd hoped to win;
And lo, the end approaches just as I
Was thinking of preparing to begin.

AN ANONYMOUS ENGLISH LAD

ONE MOTHER'S GRIEF AT THE DEATH OF A SON

Although it was brief and very strange, the feeling lasted long enough that I can recall it out of the turmoil of that terrible morning, out of my own shock, my growing sense of prickling disorientation, out of the gathering deep rumble of what would soon become my madwoman's, madmother's roaring, uncontainable grief.

Other parents who have lost children will understand the way this grief, when fully developed, changed me completely. From then on, it was as if my life had been cleaved: everything before the day of Johnny's death belonged to one person, and everything afterward to another. But the grief had not yet begun to grow, and I knew when I heard my mother's words, the morning of my son's death, that the tornado developing within me would not come out, not yet.

REEVE LINDBERGH, *Under a Wing: A Memoir* (pp. 84–85)
(Her mother and father were Col. Charles Lindbergh and Anne

Morrow Lindbergh. They too had lost a son. He was kidnapped and murdered.)

GRIEF

I have been daily grateful for the friend who remarked that grief isolates. He did not mean only that I, grieving, am isolated from you, happy. He meant also that shared grief isolates the sharers from each other. Though united in that we are grieving, we grieve differently.

NICHOLAS WOLTERSTORFF,
Lament for a Son, p. 56

Take care that you do not waste your sorrows; that you do not let the precious gifts of disappointment, pain, loss, loneliness, or similar afflictions . . . mar you instead of mending you. . . . There is no failure of life so terrible as to have the pain without the lesson, the sorrow without the softening.

HUGH BLACK

May I try to tell you again where your only comfort lies? It is not in forgetting the happy past. People bring us well meant but miserable consolations when they tell us what time will do to help our grief. We do not want to lose our grief, because our grief is bound up with our love and we could not cease to mourn without being robbed of our affections.

PHILLIPS BROOKS

Today's burden is enough; do not add to it tomorrow's. . . . Tomorrow's burden will come and soon enough, but today's burden will have been lifted before the new one is fastened upon your shoulders. . . . The burden is heavy, but God's grace is sufficient.

MRS. CHARLES COWMAN

The God of Israel, the Savior, is sometimes a God that hides Himself but never a God that absents Himself; sometimes in the dark, but never at a distance.

MATTHEW HENRY

Grief is the agony of an instant; the indulgence of grief, the blunder of a life.

BENJAMIN DISRAELI

Sorrow, however, turns out to be not a state but a process. It needs not a map but a history.

C. S. LEWIS

You never know how much you really believe anything until its truth or falsehood becomes a matter of life and death to you.

C. S. LEWIS

It's hard to have patience with people who say "There is no death" or "Death doesn't matter." There is death. And whatever is matters. And whatever happens has consequences, and it and they are irrevocable and irreversible. You might as well say that birth doesn't matter.

C. S. LEWIS

HOPE IN JESUS CHRIST

AN EASTER CAROL

Tomb, thou shalt not hold Him longer;
Death is strong, but life is stronger;
Stronger than the dark—the light;
Stronger than the wrong—the right;
Faith and hope triumphant say,
"Christ will rise on Easter Day!"

PHILLIPS BROOKS
(who also wrote "O Little Town of Bethlehem")

Those who know the way to God can find it in the dark.

ALEXANDER MACLAREN

You cannot cure your own sorrow by nursing it; the longer it is nursed, the more habitual it grows. . . . You cannot cure your sorrow by nursing it; but you can cure it by nursing another's sorrow. [See 2 Corinthians 1:4.]

GEORGE MATHESON

I accept in the darkness the burden Thou hast laid upon me; I take it unexplained.

GEORGE MATHESON

It is a solemn fact which some of us know all too well that sorrow leaves us either closer to God or farther away. It is a double-edged tool. It either scars or beautifies.

JAMES H. McCONKEY

Death may be the "king of terrors" [Job 18:14], but Jesus is the King of Kings.

DWIGHT L. MOODY

> God holds the key of all unknown,
> And I am glad;
> If other hands should hold the key,
> Or if He trusted it to me,
> I might be sad.
>
> What if tomorrow's cares were here
> Without its rest?
> I'd rather He unlocked the day;
> And as the hours swing open, say,
> "My will is best."
>
> The very dimness of my sight
> Makes me secure;
> For groping in my misty way,
> I feel His hand; I hear Him say,
> "My help is sure."
>
> I cannot read His future plans;
> But this I know:

I have the smiling of His face,
And all the refuge of His grace,
While here below.

Enough! This covers all my wants,
And so I rest!
For what I cannot, He can see,
And in His care I saved shall be,
Forever blest!

J. PARKER

Let us go forward. God leads us. Though blind, shall we be afraid to follow? I do not see my way: I do not care to: but I know that He sees His way, and that I see Him.

CHARLES KINGSLEY

HEAVEN

If you read history you will find that the Christians who did most for the present world were precisely those who thought most of the next. It is since Christians have largely ceased to think of the other world that they have become so ineffective in this.

C. S. LEWIS

Aim at heaven and you will get earth thrown in [Matthew 6:33]. Aim at earth and you will get neither.

C. S. LEWIS

Has this world been so kind to you that you should leave with regret? There are better things ahead than any we leave behind.

C. S. LEWIS

He that has gone to prepare a place for us by His presence has prepared the way to that place by His providence.

CHARLES HADDON SPURGEON

I haven't lost my wife Sara because I know where she is. You haven't lost anything when you know where it is. Death can hide but not divide.

VANCE HAVNER

There are two sides to dying—the earth side and the heaven side.

ANONYMOUS

. . . our Lord expanded life into eternity. Our life shall go on developing forever, under the sunshine and the love of God. . . . The environment of heaven shall be perfect.

GEORGE H. MORRISON

Our God does not beat down the storms that rise against Him; He rides upon them [2 Samuel 22:1]; He works through them. . . . He might have said to the storm, "Peace, be still!" But there was a more excellent way—to ride upon it. . . . You too should ride upon the wings of the wind. . . . Go out to meet the storm!

GEORGE MATHESON

Christ has made of death a narrow, starlit strip between the companionships of yesterday and the reunions of tomorrow.

WILLIAM JENNINGS BRYAN

Rebirth brings us into the kingdom of grace, and death into the kingdom of glory.

RICHARD BAXTER

This world is the land of the dying; the next is the land of the living.

TRYON EDWARDS

LAST WORDS OF FAMOUS PEOPLE

It appears that dying people often speak about the things that concerned them most in life. "For out of the overflow of the heart the mouth speaks."

MATTHEW 12:34

I shall hear in heaven.

LUDWIG VAN BEETHOVEN

Yes, yes Billy! You go down that side of Long Pond, and I'll go this side, and we'll get the ducks.

JOHN JAMES AUDUBON, to his friend Bill Bakewell

Be sure and sing "Precious Lord, Take My Hand." Sing it real pretty.

MARTIN LUTHER KING JR., to musician Ben Branch

The waters are rising, but so am I. I am not going under, but over! Do not be concerned about dying—go on living well and the dying will be right.

CATHERINE BOOTH, who with her husband, William, founded the Salvation Army

The best of all, God is with us! Farewell!

JOHN WESLEY

Earth is receding; heaven is opening. God is calling. I must go.

DWIGHT L. MOODY

Let the tent be struck!

ROBERT E. LEE

(singing) There is none in heaven
Nor on earth like Thee;
Thou hast died for sinners,
Thou hast died for me.

(folding her hands over her heart) There, now it's all over. Blessed rest!

FRANCES RIDLEY HAVERGAL

A life spent in the service of God and communion with Him is the most comfortable and pleasant life that one can live in the present world.

MATTHEW HENRY

Texas! Texas!
Margaret! [his wife]
SAM HOUSTON

Moose. Indian!
HENRY DAVID THOREAU

Turn up the lights—I don't want to go home in the dark.
O. HENRY (William Sidney Porter)

Chief of the army!
NAPOLEON I

So little done—so much to do!
CECIL RHODES

How is the Empire?
KING GEORGE II OF GREAT BRITAIN

All my possessions for a moment of time.
QUEEN ELIZABETH I OF ENGLAND

How were the receipts today at Madison Square Garden?
P. T. BARNUM

Go to the bank, Sidney [his secretary]. See if that check came in . . .
the show looks great.
FLORENZ ZIEGFELD

Ideas for Funeral Messages

W e share these brief outlines so that you may adapt, expand, and personalize them to meet the needs of the mourners to whom you minister. Meditate on the texts and the suggested outlines, and let the messages become your own so that you may speak from your own heart. Better yet, improve these messages!

GENERAL MESSAGES

When Christians die, they go to heaven:
1. Because of the price that Jesus paid—1 Thessalonians 5:9–10
2. Because of the promise that Jesus made—John 14:1–6
3. Because of the prayer that Jesus prayed—John 17:24

Before Jesus went to die for us on the cross, He shared four comforting truths with His followers. Those truths are found in John 14:1–6 (read).

1. Death is real—we must not deny it
2. Heaven is real—we must desire it
3. Salvation is real—we must receive it
4. Christ's return is real—we must expect it

THE GODLY "SENIOR SAINT"
(SIMEON, LUKE 2:25–32)

1. His death was permitted by God
2. His death followed a godly life of faithful service
3. His death meant peace—he had seen the Savior!

1. Look at his eyes: a promise was fulfilled; he saw Jesus
2. Look at his lips: he praises the Sovereign Lord
3. Look at his heart—he is experiencing God's peace
   "depart" in Greek means the releasing of a prisoner, the taking down of a tent, the setting sail of a ship, the un-yoking of a beast of burden

FOR ONE WHO SERVED THE LORD FAITHFULLY
(ACTS 13:36)

1. In life, he/she served the Lord
   David still serves the Lord—his psalms, etc.
   1 John 2:17
2. In death, he/she sleeps, awaiting resurrection (Psalm 30:5)
   [Note: the body sleeps, not the spirit]
3. In heaven, he/she enjoys rest and reward—Revelation 14:13

FOR A FAITHFUL SUNDAY SCHOOL TEACHER
(LUKE 10:38–42; JOHN 12:1–3)

1. She/he chose Christ—salvation
2. She/he chose the Word
   Explain what the Word is to the child of God: life, light, food, etc.
3. She/he chose sacrifice—John 12:1–3
4. What she/he chose will last forever

FOR SOMEONE WHO DIED ALONE

It grieves us to think that [insert name] was alone when he/she died. But in reality, he/she was not alone. The Scriptures give us these truths:

1. Christ was with him/her—Psalm 23:4
2. He/she is with Christ—2 Corinthians 5:8–9
3. Christ is now with us—Isaiah 41:10; Hebrews 13:5
4. One day, all who trust Jesus will be together—1 Thessalonians 4:13–18

SUGGESTIONS FROM OLD TESTAMENT TEXTS

2 Samuel 14:14

The woman compared death to "water spilled on the ground." That water cannot be reclaimed, and death cannot be reversed. Like David, we must take courage and accept the death of a loved one and go on living. But the spilled water is not necessarily wasted or lost. If the sun lifts it in evaporation, it will return as rain. If it seeps into the ground, it helps vegetation to grow. God has His purposes, and we can accept them by faith.

Job 23:10

The picture is that of gold put into the furnace and coming out refined for the jeweler's use. Job was suffering both sorrow (his children dead) and pain (his body diseased), but he saw his experiences as God's temporary process leading to blessing. When God puts us into His furnace, He keeps His eye on the clock (He knows how long) and His hand on the thermostat (He knows how much).

Psalm 23

This familiar psalm is about what Jesus is doing for His people (sheep) today. Note the phrase "all the days of my life" in verse 6. As we look back, we will see that God's goodness and mercy have been with us, and as we look ahead, we see the Father's house (heaven) before us. Meanwhile, the Shepherd is with us to protect and provide, and He will take us to glory. The Good Shepherd died for the sheep (John 10), and now He lives for the sheep. One day, He will come for His sheep and take them home.

Psalm 90:12 (NASB)

We measure life in years, but God tells us to measure life in days. This verse gives us some important lessons about life.

1. Life is about learning—"teach us"
2. Life is about what counts—"to number"
   What really matters most to us? Life is short and swift!
3. Life is preparation for eternity—"present to You a heart of wisdom"

We live a day at a time. Each day ends with sleep, a picture of death; each day begins with waking, a picture of resurrection. One day we shall meet God! Are we prepared?

Psalm 126:5

1. Life is a time of sowing (see Galatians 6:9)
2. Life is also a time of weeping—we water the seed with our tears
3. Through Christ, our tears can bring a harvest of joy (Psalm 30:5)

Ecclesiastes 7:1–4

Most of us would rather go to a feast than to a funeral, but Solomon advises to choose the funeral and learn from it. We get our name when we are born, and the value of that name—good or bad—is sealed at death. The deceased can't do damage to his/her name after death. A good name remains fragrant like expensive perfume. Let's not try to overcome our grief with false mirth. Rather, let's determine to build Christian character and leave behind a name that honors Christ and encourages others to follow Him.

Isaiah 43:1–5a

Grief is something we "go through"—it's a journey. God gives us four assurances that we can depend on as we make the journey.

1. God knows who we are—"I have summoned you by name"
   In our culture, we know people by numbers—telephone, e-mail, home address, etc.; but to God we are unique persons with names.

2. God knows where we are
   Overwhelmed in a flood, burned in the fire, things changing around us
3. God knows how we feel
   Afraid (vv. 1, 5)—alone vv. 2, 5)—but we are precious to Him (v. 4)
4. God knows what we need and supplies it
   To be wanted—"You are mine" (v. 1)
   To be loved—"I love you" (v. 4)
   To have hope—He sees us "through" (v. 2 twice)

Jesus went through all of this for us when He was here on earth. He died on the cross and arose from the dead, and He alone can give eternal life and the strength we need for grief's journey.

Isaiah 63:7–9

These verses affirm the truth that God is good, and because He is good, we can be sure that—

1. He knows how we feel
2. He shares in our grief
3. He gives us just the help we need

SUGGESTIONS FROM NEW TESTAMENT TEXTS

Matthew 15:4

The word "blessed" carries the idea of joy and enrichment from God.

1. We know that we hurt as we grieve
2. We know that we need help
3. We know that God's blessing will comfort us (the word "comfort" comes from the Latin and means "with strength")

Matthew 14:12—"Tell it to Jesus"

1. His ear is open to your prayers
2. His heart is moved with compassion
3. His power is able to meet your every need
4. His purposes are always perfect
   Therefore—"tell it to Jesus"

Mark 4:38—"Does Jesus care?"

The disciples were in a difficult situation. Beneath them was the sea, around them were the wind and the waves and the darkness, and behind them was Jesus—asleep! Didn't He care? But the disciples' biggest problem was not the storm on the outside but the fear on the inside, and that was caused by lack of faith. Jesus didn't prevent the storm, and Jesus wasn't afraid of the storm. *But Jesus did care!* Years later, Peter would write in his first epistle (5:7), "Cast all your anxiety upon him because he cares for you."

Luke 22:43

An angel came to the garden and strengthened Jesus. Angels are the servants of the people of God (Hebrews 1:14), and even though we don't recognize them, they come to us when—

1. We pray and seek God's face
2. We yield completely to His will—"Your will be done"
3. We step out by faith and obey the Lord

Luke 24:29—"Stay with us . . ."

Like those two discouraged men on the Emmaus road—

1. We don't always understand what God is doing
2. We don't always recognize Jesus when He comes to us
3. We can learn new truths from God's Word
4. We can have new blessings to share with others

John 11:31—Mary stopped to see Jesus before she went to her brother's grave.

1. Jesus waits for us to come
2. Jesus welcomes us with love
3. Jesus weeps with us and shares our sorrow
4. Jesus works to bring life and joy

> He is the resurrection and the life right now, so we have His life and power now as we experience sorrow.

John 11:35— "Jesus wept"

These two simple words teach us some profound truths that bring comfort to the grieving heart.

1. Jesus feels our grief
2. Jesus was strong enough to cry
3. Jesus understands why we cry
4. Jesus can turn sorrow into joy—not substitution but transformation (see John 16:21–22)

John 14:6 (Use when the deceased person's eternal destiny is unknown)

[Name of the deceased] did not speak openly about his/her faith. But this is a day when we need faith and must not be silent about it. Faith in Jesus Christ means eternal life, comfort, and peace. The text asks three questions and presents Jesus Christ as the only answer.

1. Where are you going? "I am the way"
2. What are you trusting? "I am the truth"
3. Is your life worth living? "I am the life"

John 20:13—"Why are you crying?"
1. Christ is alive, not dead
2. Christ is present, not absent
3. Christ knows your name and your needs
4. Christ in heaven today can meet those needs

Romans 8:18
1. A personal evaluation—"I consider"—the result of his experience
2. A promised transformation—from suffering to glory
3. A perfect compensation—glory for each pain and tear
   But it is only for those who have trusted Jesus Christ

Hebrews 11:21—"Leaned on the top of his staff"
1. The staff of a pilgrim—the starting point of his walk (Genesis 28:10)
2. The support of a cripple—God gave him a limp, and that was the turning point in his life (Genesis 32–33)
3. The scepter of a prince—"Israel, a prince with God" headed for glory
   What a wonderful finishing point!

FOR THE FUNERAL OF A CHILD

1.

The best place for a child is in somebody's loving arms. When Jesus was here on earth, He welcomed the children and took them into His arms. (Read Mark 10:13–16.)

But Jesus is no longer here on earth personally. He is alive in heaven, and that's even better. On earth, He could be only one place at a time, but now He is everywhere—and He is here with us.

The newspaper account said that [decedent's name] died, but we know better. [Name] was taken to heaven into the arms of Jesus. We would have preferred that [name] stay with us longer, but we won't question the plans of our Lord. We mourn because a piece of our hearts—a part of our future—has been taken from us. Someone has said that when a hero dies, there is gratitude, and when an elderly person dies, there is fulfillment, but when a baby dies, there is something wrong somewhere. What can we do?

1. We can talk to our Father and ask for the help that we need.
2. We can accept the Father's will even as Jesus did in the garden (John 18:11). Peter wanted to fight God's will; he had a sword. Jesus accepted the cup.
3. We can believe the Savior's promises (read John 14:1–6).

Jesus is coming again, and we will experience a great time of reunion. We believe that [name] will be grown up, but we'll know him and take him in our arms, just as Jesus took him in His arms. Until then, let's keep our arms around one another, sharing our love and encouragement. "The eternal God is your refuge, and underneath are the everlasting arms" (Deuteronomy 33:27 KJV).

2.

"Weeping may endure for a night, but joy comes in the morning" (Psalm 30:5 NKJV).

We have here two elements that appear in every child's life—weeping and joy. When night comes, children don't want to go to bed, so they cry. But when morning comes, they bound out of bed to face a new day joyfully and expectantly.

As parents and grandparents, we try to convince the children that sleep is important and crying is unnecessary. We assure them that the morning will bring an exciting new day. But today, it's we the adults who need to learn this message. We're the ones who are weeping as we experience this dark night of sorrow. At night we can't always see things clearly or in their right perspective, but we know that the night won't last forever and that the morning of joy will come.

As Christians, we anticipate that day when Jesus will return and the night will be swallowed up in the light of the new day. Then we will see clearly. Then we will rejoice eternally.

This precious child was put to sleep in Jesus and is now experiencing eternal day. For us, it is the night, and we're weeping. But the morning will come, and our tears will be transformed into joy. God's people will be together in the city where there are no tears.

3.

The question we're all asking is, "Why?" It's a question often asked in the Bible, but God doesn't always answer it directly. We don't always know why, but we do have certainties we can rely on to give us comfort and hope.

1. God shares in our sorrows (Isaiah 63:9)
2. This child is with Jesus (2 Samuel 12:23)
3. God's grace can and will sustain us, if we ask Him (2 Corinthians 12:9)

4.

"Like a shepherd He will tend His flock, in His arm He will gather the lambs and carry them in His bosom; He will gently lead the nursing ewes" (Isaiah 40:11 NASB).

1. Jesus the Good Shepherd guides us

   He knows what is best, so we need not question His will.
2. Jesus gathers His sheep and never loses even one
3. Jesus takes special care of the little lambs
4. Jesus also gives special care to the ewes (mothers)

5.

"For this child I prayed. . . . Therefore I also have lent him to the Lord . . . "So they worshiped the Lord there" (1 Samuel 1:28 NKJV).

1. We receive our children as God's gifts
2. We pray for our children
3. We give them back to the Lord
4. We worship the Lord, no matter what He does

FOR THE FUNERAL OF A SUICIDE

1.

"Lord, if —" (John 11:21, 32)

Two one-syllable words. One of them hurts—"if." One of them heals—"Lord." Let's begin with the one that hurts—the word "if."

If [decedent's name] had not been alone. If one of us had caught the signals soon enough. If somebody had just telephoned him at the right time. Do you know why *if* hurts? Because it looks back to a past we cannot change. It doesn't look up to the Lord and strengthen our faith. It doesn't look ahead and brighten our hope. *If* asks for explanations and, in this life, not everything will be explained. Let's face it: *if* is a selfish word that suggests that *we* are in control of things. God isn't to blame for our mistakes and bad decisions, but neither is He handicapped when we make them. He's still on the throne.

That brings us to the word that heals—*Lord.* Martha and Mary were heartbroken because their beloved brother had died, yet they called Jesus "Lord." He could have arrived sooner and intervened, but He chose to wait. He is still Lord. What kind of Lord is He?

Jesus is the *Lord of love*, and love is the medicine that heals. (See John

11:3, 5, 36.) In love Jesus came to His friends in their hour of need and gave them words of encouragement. In love Jesus wept at the tomb. Today, Jesus feels the pain that we feel, and He loves us no matter how we feel. Our faith may be small, our hopes may be dim, but He is with us and loves us. It was at the cross that He proved His love for us (Romans 5:8).

Jesus is the *Lord of life.* "I am the resurrection and the life" (John 11:25). Mary and Martha believed in a future resurrection, but Jesus told them that wherever He is, resurrection power is available. Paul had this in mind when he wrote, "That I may know Him and the power of His resurrection . . ." (Philippians 3:10 NKJV). Today, in this time of sorrow, Jesus is with us and can give us the strength we need to carry the burdens. Jesus not only raised Lazarus from the dead, but He also raised Mary and Martha from the depths of sorrow and defeat.

Jesus is the *Lord of glory.* The emphasis in this chapter is on the glory of God (John 11:4, 40). At the time, the death of Lazarus didn't seem like a glorious event, but eventually it brought glory to God and even brought sinners to faith in Christ. Yes, God can use our pain today to glorify Jesus. What looks to us like tragedy can one day result in great triumph.

For Christians, the best is yet to come. Jesus compared death to "sleep" (John 11:11), because the body sleeps as the spirit is at home with the Lord. When Christ returns, He will raise the bodies of deceased believers and bathe them in glory. If death is only sleep, then there's nothing for us to fear.

Which of these little words are we taking for ourselves? The word *if?* But that's the word that hurts. The word *Lord?* That's the word that heals. We Christians don't say, "Lord, if"; we just simply by faith say, "Lord."

2.

In 1 Corinthians 13:11–13, Paul describes two different attitudes toward life, that of a child and that of a mature adult. The child wants everything explained; the adult is willing to accept mysteries and paradoxes, darkness and questions. We must be mature as we face life, for life has its share of sorrows and tragedies. Two words Paul uses help us to understand and accept the difficult burdens and problems of life. They are "now" and "then."

I. Now

    1. We wish our "now" were different, but we cannot change it

    2. We cannot see what it means, but the Lord knows

    3. We do know that God loves us and cares for us, and we will trust Him

II. Then

    1. There is a "then"—death is not the end

    2. What a bright future we have in Christ!

    From the partial to the complete

    From the passing to the eternal

    From vague reflections to full recognition

For the unexplained mysteries, we have faith in Christ.
For the wounds of disappointment, we have hope in Christ.
For our loneliness and emptiness, we have love in and from Christ.

3.

Read Romans 8:38–39 and Luke 19:10.

Death separates us from people we love, and that separation makes us grieve. But Paul tells us that death cannot separate us from the love of God as experienced in our Lord Jesus Christ! What kind of love is the love of God?

    1. It is a love that seeks—Jesus is the Good Shepherd (Luke 19:10)

    2. It is a love that saves—Jesus is the Savior (Luke 19:10)

    3. It is a love that keeps—Romans 8:38–39

Have you experienced the love of God in Jesus?

Bibliography

Baby boomers are moving from applauding The Grateful Dead to worrying about a graceless death," wrote Marvin Olasky in his article "Whistling Past the Graveyard" (*World* magazine, July/August 2002), in which he provides a helpful annotated bibliography of some newer books that deal with the subject of death. We recommend his bibliography to you. Death was once a taboo topic in American publishing, but of late it has become quite popular and publishers are taking advantage of this new interest, and this includes Christian publishers.

Our bibliography includes titles both new and old, some of which are no longer in print but are worth searching for and adding to your library. The inclusion of a title does not mean that we agree with everything in it, but only that the book is worth reading if you want know more about death and bereavement. We have learned a great deal from people we disagree with, and this has helped us know better how to minister to them when they attend the funeral service.

PERSONAL MEMOIRS

Albom, Mitch. *Tuesdays with Morrie*. New York: Doubleday, 1997. A dying professor and a former student meet weekly and chat about life and death and take the usual humanistic views of both. This has been a best seller for years, so you had better read it, but it doesn't contain much solid help you can share with the dying patient who wants some assurance for life after death. Morrie

Schwartz also wrote his own book, *Letting Go: Morrie's Reflections on Living While Dying.* New York: Bantam Doubleday Dell, 1996. It's another collection of familiar humanistic aphorisms.

Attlee, Rosemary. *William's Story.* Wheaton: Harold Shaw, 1983. A mother's account of the life and death of her athletic teenage son and how God helped both of them cope. More than half of the book is devoted to William's personal journal of his last four months of life.

Aulds, Danny and Karen. *"My Grace Is Sufficient": A Story of God's Grace in the Midst of AIDS.* A tainted blood transfusion gave Danny AIDs, but he didn't know it until after he had married Karen. Danny died in 1995. Both were Christian believers and experienced God's grace in remarkable ways. A well-written account that will help AIDS victims and their families. Privately printed, the book is available from: The Face of AIDs Ministry, P.O. Box 7781, Oxford, AL 36203.

Bernardin, Joseph Cardinal. *The Gift of Peace: Personal Reflections.* Chicago: Loyola Press, 1997. A Roman Catholic leader tells of his ministry to cancer patients and how he dealt with the cancer that eventually took his life. He also discusses the false accusations made against him and how he forgave his accuser,

Brouwer, Arie. *Overcoming the Threat of Death: A Journal of One Christian's Encounter with Cancer.* Grand Rapids: Eerdmans, 1994. Ten "reflections" from a church leader's journal, plus two sermons, point the way to faith and assurance in times of crisis.

Doka, Kenneth J. ed. *Living with Grief After Sudden Loss.* Washington, DC: Hospice Foundation of America, 1996. A compilation of excellent essays to assist you in understanding and responding to every type of sudden loss.

Evans, Jocelyn (pseud.). *Living with a Man Who's Dying.* New York: Taplinger, 1971. A wife's record of the problems she faced with the medical profession because her husband, who had cancer, wanted to die in peace at home. Neither professed any kind of religious faith.

Gunther, John. *Death Be Not Proud: A Memoir.* New York: Harper, 1949; Harper and Row paperback, 1965. The well-known American journalist (1901–1970) and author of the popular *Inside* books (*Inside Africa, Inside Russia Today,* etc.) tells how his son Johnny lived with a brain tumor and then died at age seventeen. Selections from Johnny's letters and diaries help us understand how this teenager faced death. A classic account of a seeming tragedy, but it provides very few answers.

Kooiman, Gladys. *When Death Takes a Father.* Grand Rapids: Baker, 1968; paperback edition, 1974. A beautifully written book about the faith of a family and how a brave widow and mother learned personally that God really does care.

Neuhaus, Richard John. *As I Lay Dying: On Facing Death and Living Again.* New York: Basic Books, 2002. Dr. Neuhaus, the well-known former Lutheran pastor and now Roman Catholic priest, came to the brink of death and was brought back to tell us about it. "Death eludes explanation," he writes. "Death is the death of explanation." But his book contains insights that can help us encourage others and ourselves.

Wolterstoff, Nicholas. *Lament for a Son.* Grand Rapids: Eerdmans, 1987. A famous philosopher and educator lays bare his heart and shares the wisdom and insights that encouraged him as he grieved the death of a son.

DEATH—GENERAL VIEWS

Becker, Ernest. *The Denial of Death.* New York: Free Press, 1973. Awarded a Pulitzer Prize for this book, anthropologist Ernest Becker examines the place of death in Freud's system of psychoanalysis and the struggle Freud had in dealing with it personally and professionally. Not a book to skim but to be studied thoughtfully.

Carlozzi, Carl G. *Death and Contemporary Man: The Crisis of Terminal Illness.* Grand Rapids: Eerdmans, 1968. The author is a Christian minister and a hospital chaplain. In this brief but adequate book, he discusses how patients and their families, pastors, and doctors look at terminal illness, and how we may minister to terminal patients.

Christakis, Nicholas A. *Death Foretold: Prophecy and Prognosis in Medical Care*. Chicago and London: University of Chicago Press, 1999. An inside look at the pressures doctors face when patients ask about their future. The author explains how doctors assess the data and seek to mix expertise with compassion as they reflect on each patient's situation. The book emphasizes the importance of a healthy relationship between physician and patient and the importance of seeing the disease, not the doctor, as the enemy.

Chroron, Jacques. *Death and Western Thought*. New York: Collier Books, 1963. An excellent survey of the views of death presented by major branches of philosophy. Expect many questions, some excellent quotations, but not many solid answers.

Feldman, Fred. *Confrontations with the Reaper: A Philosophical Study of the Nature and Value of Death*. New York: Oxford University Press, 1992. An author who affirms that "death is a mystery" calmly looks at death from a philosophical point of view and concludes that "understanding death" is the best way to prepare for death.

Fitzgerald, Helen. *The Mourning Handbook*. New York: Simon and Schuster, 1994. A no-nonsense topical question-and-answer approach to grief that deals with emotional problems, relationships, complications, and other matters relating to grief. The section on recovery is thorough but lacks a Christian perspective.

Garland, Robert. *The Greek Way of Death*. Ithica, NY: Cornell University Press, 1985. An excellent survey of what the Greeks believed about death and the afterlife and how they buried their dead. Excellent documentation.

Grollman, Earl A. ed. *Concerning Death: A Practical Guide for the Living*. Boston: Beacon 1974. Using a question-and-answer approach, experts present twenty essays on various aspects of death, from the care of the dying person to selecting a cemetery plot and designing a headstone. Somewhat dated but still helpful.

Hardt, Dale V. *Death the Final Frontier*. Englewood Cliffs, NJ: Prentice-Hall, 1979. Examines various "attitudes" toward death as revealed by statistical studies based on answers to twenty questions. Shares helpful miscellaneous data.

Hendin, David. *Death as a Fact of Life.* New York: Norton, 1973; reprint Warner Books, 1974. A science journalist seeks to help answer questions people may have when confronted by the death of a loved one. What is "legal death"? How do doctors respond when patients die? Are we allowed to grieve? How do children look at death? Practical and well written.

Kastenbaum, Robert, and Beatrice Kastenbaum. *The Encyclopedia of Death.* New York: Avon Books, 1993. This is a helpful volume that contains articles about many aspects of death, both ancient and contemporary, religious and secular, medical and cultural. The articles are concise but adequate and deal with many different religions.

Kauffman, Walter. *Existentialism, Religion and Death.* New York: New American Library, 1976. At one time professor of philosophy at Princeton University, Kauffman critiques the systems of leading existentialists from Kierkegaard to Martin Buber and applies their views to religion, death, and the Jewish people.

Kilner, John F., Arlene B. Miller, and Edmund D. Pellegrino, eds. *Dignity and Dying: A Christian Appraisal.* Grand Rapids: Eerdmans, 1996. A collection of concise essays that cover a broad spectrum of issues relating to death and dying. It has excellent definitions of key terms in the vocabulary of thanatology. While a bit dated, it is still a valuable resource to keep handy for ready reference.

Kreeft, Peter. *Love Is Stronger than Death.* San Francisco: Ignatius, 1992. Christian philosopher Peter Kreeft uses the Bible to illumine five images of death: the enemy, the stranger, the friend, the mother, and the lover. The book is theological, philosophical, and pastoral. A must read.

Kubler-Ross, Elisabeth. *Death: The Final Stage of Growth.* New York: Simon and Schuster, 1975. An anthology of essays on death, only two of them by Kubler-Ross. We wonder where she gets her optimistic view of the afterlife.

McCane, Byron M. *Roll Back the Stone: Death and Burial in the World of Jesus.* Harrisburg, PA: Trinity Press, 2003. A clear presentation of funeral practices in early Roman Palestine and how they impinge on the burial of Jesus.

Moller, David Wendell. *Confronting Death: Values, Institutions and Human Mortality*. New York: Oxford University Press, 1996. A university professor of sociology examines what modern technology and "professionalism" have done to "dehumanize the experience of death." Are doctors in control of death and morticians in control of funerals? Do mourning people need professional grief therapists? What is the place of religion in all of this? Dr. Moller raises the issues and deals with them skillfully, but doe not present any encouraging answers for the dying.

Nuland, Sherwin B. *How We Die: Reflections on Life's Final Chapter*. New York: Knopf, 1994. Dr. Nuland is a surgeon and a teacher of surgeons, as well as a capable writer, and in this book he describes how different kinds of diseases take life away from people. After reading it, you won't be able to say to dying patients "I know just how you feel," but you will better appreciate what they are enduring and what the medical staff is doing for them.

Nyberg, Dorothea Martin. *Life Support: Christian Compassion and the Terminally Ill*. San Bernardino, CA.: Here's Life, 1988. In spite of its publication date, the book addresses contemporary situations with accuracy. It clearly defines medical and legal terms and illustrates them from real life. The information for both patients and caregivers is ample and helpful.

Parrish-Harra, Carol W. *A New Age Handbook on Death and Dying*. Marina del Rey, CA: Devorss, 1982. Based on mystical Eastern religions, vague sentimentality, out-of-body reports, and other tenuous foundations, the book teaches denial rather than facing reality and false assurance rather than confidence. But, alas, many people have the New Age mind-set, so let's find out what they think.

Stennard, David E. *The Puritan Way of Death*. New York: Oxford University Press, 1977. A careful study of New England family and community life as reflected in the Puritans' attitudes toward death and burial and how these views affect ideas of death in contemporary America.

Taylor, John H. *Death and the Afterlife in Ancient Egypt*. London: British Museum Press, 2001. Taylor is the assistant keeper in the

Department of Egyptian Antiquities in the British Museum. He carefully explains what the ancient Egyptians believed and how it governed their burial practices. Lavishly illustrated, this is the best volume on ancient Egyptian theology and eschatology for the general student.

Thielicke, Helmut. *Living with Death*. Grand Rapids: Eerdmans, 1983. The distinguished German professor and preacher focuses on the theology of death and how the biblical message relates to life today. He raises and answers some questions most of us would not ask because we have never gone that deep into the subject.

Wolf, Richard. *The Last Enemy*. Washington, DC: Canon Press, 1974. An excellent brief study of important topics, including how people evade the fact of death, death in Eastern and Western traditions, and the Bible and suicide, all from the evangelical Christian perspective.

DEATH IN JEWISH CULTURE

Gillman, Neil. *The Death of Death: Resurrection and Immortality in Jewish Thought*. Woodstock, VT: Jewish Lights, 1997. A noted Jewish theologian comes out for resurrection and immortality and uses the Bible and quotations from Jewish thinkers to strengthen his case.

Kolatch, Alfred J. *The Jewish Mourner's Book of Why*. Middle Village, NY: Jonathan David, 1996. Rabbi Kolatch explains Jewish beliefs and practices and includes all Jewish denominations. A rich source of information presented with compassion and skill.

Lamm, Maurice. *The Jewish Way in Death and Mourning*. Middle Village, NY: Jonathan David; revised edition, 1977. Presents and defends the orthodox Jewish views of death, funerals, burials, and mourning practices.

Riemer, Jack, ed. *Jewish Reflections on Death*. New York: Schocken Books, 1974. A collection of articles and essays relating to death in the Jewish culture, most of which have application to death in other cultures.

FUNERAL DIRECTORS

Laderman, Gary. *Rest in Peace: A Cultural History of Death and the Funeral Home in Twentieth-Century America.* New York: Oxford University Press, 2003. An authoritative and balanced study, including his evaluation of Jessica Mitford's crusade against "the funeral industry." The author's view of the future of funerals and funeral homes is worth considering.

Lynch, Thomas. *Bodies In Motion and At Rest: On Metaphor and Mortality.* New York: Norton, 2000. A collection of essays on many topics from poet and professional undertaker Thomas Lynch, who feels it's time the undertakers had their say.

———. *The Undertaking: Life Studies from the Dismal Trade.* New York: Norton, 1997. This is Lynch's first collection of essays. With grace and humor, he gives the other side of the story.

Mitford, Jessica. *The American Way of Death Revisited.* New York: Knopf, 1998. A revision of the 1963 edition that updates statistics and includes new material. It's interesting to read her evaluation of the responses of the "funeral industry" to the first edition of the book. Most funeral directors have read the book, so pastors and other caregivers ought to read it too, if only to be conversant with the situation.

THE AFTERLIFE

Alcorn, Randy. *Heaven.* Wheaton: Tyndale, 2004. An easy-to-read compendium of biblical truth that from a biblical viewpoint answers many of the questions people ask about heaven. You may not agree with all the views expressed, but you must agree that the author did his homework. Highly recommended.

———. *In Light of Eternity.* Colorado Springs: WaterBrook, 1999. A smaller and earlier book presenting similar material in a concise and nonacademic way. Ideal for giving to grieving people.

Boettner, Loraine. *Immortality.* Grand Rapids: Eerdmans, 1956. An esteemed Reformed theologian brings a wealth of biblical knowledge to the discussion of three key topics: physical death, immortality, and the intermediate state. This is a basic book for the Christian caregiver who wants to know what the Bible teaches.

Brooke, Tal. *The Other Side of Death.* Wheaton: Tyndale, 1979. A sane and practical account of what Elisabeth Kubler-Ross, Raymond Moody, the Eastern mystics, and the New Age followers say about life after death and how the Scriptures answer them. The author at one time was a practicing Hindu.

Geisler, Norman L., and J. Yutaka Amano. *The Reincarnation Sensation.* Wheaton: Tyndale, 1987. As they refute the doctrine of reincarnation, two theologians expose the fallacies of Eastern mysticism and Western fascination with the "out-of-body" revelations and other New Age ideas. A solid piece of theological writing.

Gilmore, John. *Probing Heaven: Key Questions on the Hereafter.* Grand Rapids: Baker, 1989. The author combines biblical truth with philosophical perception and a keen understanding of the theological issues involved. Highly recommended.

Habermas, Gary R., and J. P. Moreland. *Beyond Death: Exploring the Evidence for Immortality [second edition].*Wheaton: Crossway, 1998. Two professional philosophers and theologians deal with the biblical foundations for immortality and answer the claims of the "near-death experience" people. They explain the believer's experience between death and the eternal state, the reality of heaven and hell, and the fallacy of reincarnation. Best of all, they apply these truths to how Christians ought to live today. This book is a must for every serious minister and caregiver. Without evading issues, it answers the questions and refutes the claims of the many false teachers.

Johnson, Christopher J., and Marsha G. McGee. *Encounter with Eternity: Religious Views of Death and Life After Death.* New York: Philosophical Library, 1986. Specialists from fifteen religious traditions share their basic beliefs about death and the afterlife. The material is summarized in an appendix.

Kreeft, Peter. *Everything You Ever Wanted to Know About Heaven but Never Dreamed of Asking.* San Francisco: Ignatius, 1990. Heaven is seen from the viewpoint of a Roman Catholic philosopher and theologian. In whatever he writes, Kreeft makes you think and manages to enlarge your intellectual horizons.

LaHaye, Tim. *Life in the Afterlife: What Really Happens After Death?* Wheaton: Tyndale, 1980. This is a careful examination of the "out-of-body" reports, plus biblical studies on death, the intermediate state, resurrection, and life in eternity.

Lewis, James R. *The Death and Afterlife Book: The Encyclopedia of Death, Near Death, and Life After Death.* Canton, MI: Visible Ink Press, 2001. Over four hundred pages of information about the people, teachings, objects, and practices of the religions and para-religious groups that focus on occult and other experiences. Excellent index. It's hard to believe that some of these things are believed in our modern world. This is a fine reference work to consult if you encounter such teachings.

MacArthur, John. *The Glory of Heaven: The Truth About Heaven, Angels and Eternal Life.* Wheaton: Crossway, 1996. Rather than giving us a detailed tour, the well-known expositor provides a biblical overview of heaven and then adds four sermons on heaven by godly preachers of the past.

McDannell, Colleen, and Bernhard Lang. *Heaven: A History.* Beginning with the ancient Jews and coming up to contemporary Christianity, the book surveys what has been taught about heaven over the centuries.

Moody, Raymond A. *Life After Life.* New York: Bantam Books, 1976. This is the "outstanding best seller" that helped to accelerate the "out-of-body" studies. The author says that "commitments to others prevent me from giving names and clarifying details" (page 176), so the approach is less than scientific. But you ought to read it if only to give then other side a fair hearing and be able to refute it.

Sanders, J. Oswald. *Heaven—Better by Far.* Grand Rapids: Discovery House, 1994. A concise manual that will enlighten and encourage. An ideal book for the caregiver to give to a mourner.

Scroggie, W. Graham. *What About Heaven?* London: Pickering and Inglis, 1940. A former pastor of Spurgeon's Tabernacle in

London, and a gifted Bible student, Scroggie wastes no words but gets to the point and stays within the bounds of Scripture.

Smith, Wilbur M. *The Biblical Doctrine of Heaven.* Chicago: Moody, 1968. In his day, Smith was recognized for his incredible knowledge of the relevant literature on biblical subjects, and the book of the Revelation was one of his specialties. This book deals with the usual topics and provides helpful quotations from many ancient and modern sources.However, it is not as practical as Alcorn, Gilmore and MacArthur.

Wiersbe, Warren W., ed. *Classic Sermons on Heaven and Hell.* Grand Rapids: Kregel, 1994.

Wright, Leoline L. *Reincarnation: A Lost Chord in Modern Thought.* Wheaton: Theosophical Publishing, 1975. The official position on reincarnation.

Wright, Rusty. *The Other Side of Life.* San Bernardino, CA: Here's Life, 1979. An excellent popular guide to what the Bible says about death and how it applies to the "out-of-body" claims and other fads. A strong evangelistic tool geared to the university crowd.

EUTHANASIA

Blocher, Mark. *The Right to Die? Caring Alternatives to Euthanasia.* Chicago: Moody, 1999. The director of the Southern Baptist Center for Biblical Bioethics deals with the elusive meaning of "death with dignity" and "assisted suicide" and explains the Christian approach to ministering to terminal patients. This is a valuable and authoritative contribution to the debate.

Fournier, Keith A., and William D. Watkins. *In Defense of Life: Taking A Stand Against the Culture of Death.* Colorado Springs.: NavPress, 1996. An excellent basic text on how today's culture views death and what natural law, civil law, and God's law say about these views.

Lynne, Joann, ed. *By No Extraordinary Means.* Bloomington, IN: Indiana University Press, 1989. Twenty-seven essays on the legal, ethical, medical, and practical aspects of euthanasia. Why not forgo food and water? What about the unconscious patient?

"There are no easy answers" seems to be the conclusion of the matter, but there are many voices giving their opinions. The book does not take a religious point of view.

Smith, Shirley Ann. *Hospice Concepts: A Guide to Palliative Care in Terminal Illness.* Champaign, IL: Research Press, 2000. The hospice movement began in Great Britain and has brought hope and comfort to many terminally ill patients. This manual is for people aspiring to serve as hospice caregivers and contains much material that is applicable to the work of Christian ministry. Chapters on spiritual care, Kubler-Ross's "stages in dying," the dying child, the use of medication, and the legal rights of the patient are especially helpful. Highly recommended.

GRIEF COUNSELING

Attig, Thomas. *How We Grieve: Relearning the World.* New York: Oxford University Press, 1996. A former professor of philosophy and specialist in death education uses case histories to illustrate principles of "active grieving" that help mourners move toward relearning the meaning of life, the world, and choice. Grieving is not a passive experience but an active process of decision making that can be guided by sympathetic caregivers.

Bregman, Lucy. *Beyond Silence and Denial: Death and Dying Reconsidered.* Louisville: Westminster John Knox, 1999. A study of the "death awareness movement" (Kubler-Ross) and the importance of the church learning and benefiting from it. The author believes that much "religious speech" is a denial of the reality of death and therefore may do more harm than good. Her key question is, "What is the role of death in the Christian faith?" and she gives some good answers. Provacative.

Harwell, Amy. *Ready to Live: Prepared to Die.* Wheaton: Harold Shaw, 1995. While basically a manual to assist individuals in planning what they want to happen to them after they die, there is much in these pages that can greatly help the caregiver counsel people who are in denial or who are facing death. "Once we are well-prepared to die, we are really freed to live," is the author's philosophy. The "Ready to Live Checklist" is a helpful tool for helping people make wise decisions about their future. The book deals with matters related to health care, insurance, funeral arrangements, "unfinished business" with family and friends, etc. Having wrestled with cancer herself, the author writes with compassion and practical wisdom.

Jackson, Edgar N. *The Many Faces of Grief.* Nashville: Abingdon, 1977. A recognized expert in grief therapy, Dr. Jackson explains the complexity of grief and then shows how it affects many areas of life. (There is even a chapter on "Grief and Sex.") Though an older book, it deals with fundamentals that do not change.

————. *Understanding Grief.* Nashville: Abingdon, 1957. One of the older books on grief that is still helpful. Jackson was one of the pioneers in the field.

Kolf, June Cerza. *When Will I Stop Hurting? Dealing with a Recent Death.* Grand Rapids: Baker, 1987. Only fifty-seven pages long, this is a fine book to put into the hands of grieving people to assure them that their grief is normal and that they can get their lives back together again. An experienced hospice staff member, the author writes with tenderness, tough love, and plenty of knowledge.

Kubler-Ross, Elisabeth. *On Death and Dying.* New York: Macmillan, 1969. This is the standard text on the "five stages" in the experience of the average terminal patient. It's based on the author's personal interviews with the patients.

Rando, Therese A. *Grief, Dying, and Death: Clinical Interventions for Caregivers.* Champaign, IL: Research Press, 1984. Though it does not take a religious point of view, this is still the closest thing to the "ultimate manual" on the subject that we have seen. Beginning with "Our Attitudes Towards Death," the book goes on to discuss grief reaction, various "bereavement situations," the funeral, the dying patient (several chapters), the dying child, and the personal concerns of caregivers. In almost five hundred pages, the author has assembled data from many sources to help us better understand the subject and better do the job.

Schiff, Harriet Sarnoff. *Living Through Mourning: Finding Comfort and Hope When a Loved One Has Died.* New York: Viking Penguin, 1986. The author walks us through the "pathways" we must trod as we move toward the acceptance of loss: sorrow, denial, anger, guilt, depression, powerlessness, unbelief. An excellent manual if you want to form a grief support group. You will have to add the faith factor.

Staudacher, Carol. *Men and Grief.* Oakland: New Harbinger, 1991. Written both for caregivers and those to whom they minister, this book answers the question, "Do men have their own way of grieving?" The answer is, yes. One counseling approach does not fit all. The author discusses the influence of boyhood experiences on adult male grief, the differences between grieving the loss of a mate and of a child, how fathers can help their children grow through grief, and how men can help other men grieve in a mature way that brings ultimate healing.

Sullender, R. Scott. *Grief and Growth.* Mahwah, NJ: Paulist, 1985. A Presbyterian minister and an accredited counselor, the author helps the pastor understand the dynamics of grief and the importance of faith and fellowship in the healing process. It is good to find a manual that emphasizes the vital place of the church in grief counseling.

Westberg, Granger E. *Good Grief.* Philadelphia: Fortress, 1962. This little book by a Lutheran minister and member of a medical school faculty has been a road map to recovery for many grieving people. Westberg sees ten stages in healthy grief recovery and explains each of them clearly and compassionately. You will like the "we" approach of the pastor as opposed to the frequent "you" approach of the average how-to manual.

THE FUNERAL

Blackwood, Andrew W. *The Funeral: A Source Book for Ministers.* Philadelphia: Westminster, 1942. Don't let that publishing date deceive you. Blackwood was chair of the practical department at Princeton Seminary for many years and knew how to separate the "trendy" from the timeless. Though a few of the suggestions may seem old-fashioned to you, the principles in this book are still applicable. During all our years of pastoral ministry, this has been to us the most helpful single book on the funeral.

Book of Common Worship. Louisville: Westminster/John Knox, 1993. A classic liturgical resource providing Sunday and daily lectionary Scripture readings, plus prayers and other helps for each Sunday and each season of the church year. The section on the Christian funeral is superb.

DEATH: A Sourcebook About Christian Death. Chicago: Liturgy Training, Archdiocese of Chicago, 1990. A fine compilation of Scripture readings, prayers, poetry, and memoirs grounded in the Roman Catholic tradition but containing many nuggets valuable to the evangelical pastor.

Irion, Paul E. *The Funeral and the Mourner.* Nashville: Abingdon, 1954. Published a decade before Jessica Mitford's *The American Way of Death,* this book explains the rationale of the Christian funeral and relates the funeral service to the pastor's personal ministry to the mourners.

————. *The Funeral: Vestige or Value?* Nashville: Abingdon, 1966. This book came out three years after the Mitford volume and defends the importance of the funeral service in contemporary society. The author recognized emerging "new designs" for funerals but urges us not to forget the original Christian meaning of this service. He identifies and examines three basic types: the religious funeral, the pseudoreligious, and the humanistic. His insights are helpful today.

Llewellyn, John F. *Saying Goodbye Your Way.* Glendale, CA: Tropico Press, 2004. The president of Forest Lawn Memorial-Parks and Mortuaries brings out of thirty years' experience the guidance most people need about caskets, burial plots, funeral options, flowers, memorials, and a host of other areas of decision.

DEATH AND CHILDREN

Dodd, Robert V. *Helping Children Cope with Death.* Scottdale, PA: Herald, 1984. A down-to-earth guidebook that can be used by parents, teachers, and pastors. The author encourages us to share the Christian perspective in a Christian manner as the child is ready for it.

Fitzgerald, Helen. *The Grieving Child: A Parent's Guide.* New York: Simon and Schuster, 1992. Excellent resources for parents who seek comfort for themselves and to share with their family. She uses the same topical question-and-answer approach as in *The Mourning Handbook.*

Kubler-Ross, Elisabeth. *On Children and Death.* New York: Macmillan, 1983. While every chapter contains ideas you need to understand and grapple with, the statistics are dated and the Christian faith gets short shrift.

McCracken, Anne, and Mary Semel. *A Broken Heart Still Beats: After Your Child Dies.* Center City, MN: Hazelden, 1998. An anthology selected by two mothers traveling on the road of grief. There are no trite selections here and many are more potent than the reader may expect.

Schiff, Harriet Sarnoff. *The Bereaved Parent.* NY: Penguin Books, 1978. This is a classic discussion by one who herself is a bereaved parent. That it has remained in print so long is evidence of its practical value. This is required reading for caregivers.

Wiersbe, David W. *Gone but Not Lost: Grieving the Death of a Child.* Grand Rapids: Baker, 1992. A series of brief biblical chapters that help to lead grieving parents through the valley. These chapters could be read as devotional meditations.

SUICIDE

Alverez, A. *The Savage God: A Study of Suicide.* New York: Random-House, 1972. The author, who himself attempted suicide, seeks to answer the question "Why do these things happen?" but confesses that he has no answers. The emphasis is on suicide as recorded in literature and he begins with Sylvia Plath, the gifted poet who took her own life, and continues with Dante, John Donne ("No man is an island . . ."), and William Cowper the hymn writer, who tried to take his life four times. As a study of suicide, the book is fascinating and insightful, but it presents no answers.

Blackburn, Bill. *What You Should Know About Suicide.* Waco: Word, 1982. A helpful manual that deals with the key questions and seeks to provide biblical answers. The author is an experienced counselor of suicidal people.

Byers, Dale A. *Suicide: How God Sustained a Family.* Schaumburg, IL: Regular Baptist, 1991. When a son committed suicide, Pastor Byers and his family had to take brave steps of faith, and they experienced God's deeper sustaining power. A fine book for families that have been devastated by a suicide and for caregivers who want to help such families.

Coleman, William. *Understanding Suicide.* Elgin, IL: Cook, 1979. The author covers the basics and offers good pastoral counsel. The chapter "After the Attempt" is especially helpful. An older book but a good one.

Demy, Timothy J., and Gary P. Stewart, eds. *Suicide: A Christian Response.* Grand Rapids: Kregel, 1998. Here are nearly five hundred pages of valuable information and counsel from people who are not only experts in their fields but also Christian believers. The writers provide legal and medical information but also share philosophical and theological reflections and wise pastoral counsel. They also discuss euthanasia. This book should be in your library.

Duckworth, Marion. *Why Teens Are Killing Themselves.* San Bernardino, CA: Here's Life, 1987. Though an older book, it still offers insights and good answers to the questions and excellent resources for preventing suicide.

Dykstra, Robert. *She Never Said Good-bye.* Wheaton: Harold Shaw, 1989. Without warning, the author's wife took her own life. She left no message and he had to struggle with sorrow, anger, and perplexity. The book throbs with the realities of life and death.

Giovacchini, Peter. *The Urge to Die: Why Young People Commit Suicide.* New York: Macmillan, 1981. A psychiatrist who specialized in treating adolescent problems helps us face facts about the hidden and not-so-hidden causes of suicides among young people. He deals with issues of freedom, depression, values, deception, and faith. "The adolescent needs something to believe in, something with deep, enduring value," he writes. "In our society he finds little to believe in" (p. 50).

Hendin, Herbert. *Suicide in America.* New York: Norton, 1982. A psychiatrist experienced in treating suicidal patients examines the contributions made to the problem by society in general, including violence, alcoholism and narcotics, the sensational press reports, and the instability of families.

Hewett, John H. *After Suicide.* Philadelphia: Westminster, 1980. A practical guide for the family and close friends of someone who has committed suicide. Outlines the seven stages in acute grief, and also tells how to explain suicide to children.

Kirk, William G. *Adolescent Suicide.* Champaign, IL: Research Press, 1993. Written primarily for middle school and high school educators and counselors, the book focuses on how to assess the student's risks of suicide, how to intervene, and how to detect causes. The author suggests training a "school crisis team." There's no reason why such a team would not work in a church's ministry as well.

Menninger, Karl. *Man Against Himself.* New York: Harcourt, Brace and World, 1938. This is the classic work on the psychology of suicide, written by a pioneer American psychiatrist. He sought to answer the question, "Why do people hate themselves and seek to destroy themselves?" You don't speed-read this book.

Quinnett, Paul G. *Suicide: The Forever Decision.* New York: Continuum, 1987. A concerned psychologist practices tough love as he writes directly to the person contemplating suicide or the one who has tried and failed. Without posturing as a judge or prosecuting attorney, he helps the reader think through what suicide is, why the person may have considered it, and what the myths and the real options are. The last chapter on "A Philosophy of Life" is a natural for leading into sharing the gospel of Jesus Christ. There is no strong spiritual message in this fine book but the wise Christian counselor can easily use Scripture to buttress the wealth of material shared.

Schneidman, Edwin S. *The Suicidal Mind.* New York: Oxford University Press, 1996. A former professor of thanatology and the founder of the American Association of Suicidology, Dr. Schneider shares psychological insights, case histories, and medical data that help us understand ourselves, our counselees, and the situations surrounding would-be suicides. "In the vast majority of suicide, the clues were there."

Stone, Howard W. *Suicide and Grief.* Philadelphia: Fortress, 1972. The author explains the differences between "normal grief" and grief over a suicide, and how the counselor must respond. He also instructs us on how to recognize and prevent suicide and how to counsel the suicide survivor.

MISCELLANEOUS RESOURCES

Many books have been published to help mourners deal with sorrow and death, and many others have been published about the deaths of famous people, what they did and what they said. All of these biographical books and quotation books must be used carefully because many myths have grown up around some of these famous people and even the most careful compiler or editor could be led astray.

Cole, Thomas R., and Mary G. Winkler. *The Oxford Book of Aging.* New York: Oxford University Press, 1994. A helpful anthology with material on the stages of life we experience as we get older and move toward death. Read it and mark the items that help you the most.

Copeland, Cyrus M. *Farewell, Godspeed: The Greatest Eulogies of Our Time.* New York: Harmony Books, 2003. Friends and relatives extol the virtues of the deceased and occasionally give us inside information. Again, read it and mark the sentences that you can use in sharing the Word. Your congregations will recognize most of these people.

Cowman, Mrs. Charles E. *Consolation*. Los Angeles: Cowman, 1950. A veteran missionary and mature Christian, Mrs. Cowman compiled this book of daily devotionals out of her wide reading and challenging experiences as a missionary and a widow. As you read, get the message in your own heart and then study how to relate it to your people today.

Enright, D. J. ed. *The Oxford Book of Death*. New York: Oxford University Press, 1983. A very helpful compilation that covers attitudes toward death, suicide, mourning, graveyards, resurrection, war, children, and a host of other topics. Read, evaluate, mark, and use.

Forbes, Malcolm, with Jeff Bloch. *They Went That-a-Way: How the Famous, the Infamous and the Great Died*. New York: Simon and Schuster, 1988. The editor selected 175 people and described the facts and the significance of the death of each. If you use any of these stories in a sermon, you may have to explain who some of the people are. There arises a generation that knows not Joseph or Ambrose Bierce or even Rudolph Valentino.

Moffat, Mary Jane, ed. *In the Midst of Winter: Selections from the Literature of Mourning*. New York: Random, 1982. A fine selection of literature from the poetry and prose of the past, taken from many different cultures. The sections in the book follow the "seasons" experienced in mourning.

Oden, Thomas C. *Classical Pastoral Care* (4 vols.). Grand Rapids: Baker, 1994. A careful theologian and a wise pastor, Oden has culled gems of truth from the church fathers, as well as recent Christian masters. The books are organized by topics and very easy to use. In a day when too many people view the church as a business to control instead of spiritual family to care for, Oden clearly explains both the why and the how of the shepherd's ministry. Volume 4 deals thoroughly with matters relating to death and grief. We cannot recommend these book too highly.

Schneidman, Edwin S. *Voices of Death*. New York: Harper and Row, 1980. A former professor of thanatology and a suicide specialist tells us what people experienced as they faced death. He quotes widely from personal documents and seeks to encourage us to face death realistically. You will discover how Hubert Humphrey dealt with impending death from cancer, and you will read the letter abolitionist John Brown wrote to his wife as he faced execution (hanging). The author presents some helpful insights.

Siegel, Marvin. *The Last Word: The* New York Times *Book of Obituaries and Farewells.* New York: William Morrow, 1997. The obituary column in the *New York Times* has long majored on celebrating life rather than announcing death. These people were better known to New Yorkers than to the average citizens in other cities, but each obituary usually presents a timeless message. Read about "The Saloonkeeper with a Soul," "Babe Ruth's Little Sick Pal," and "Angel on the High-Wire."

Terkel, Studs. *Will the Circle Be Unbroken? Reflections on Death, Rebirth, and Hunger for a Faith.* New York: New Press, 2001. Chicago's beloved journalist-philosopher interviews all sorts of people —doctors, police officers, a Hiroshima survivor, clergymen, retired teachers, musicians, an AIDS caseworker, and even a comedian—and talks about their attitudes toward life and death. He discovers a variety of both fears and faiths. Terkel knows where the heart of a matter lies, and he writes for the reader's heart.

Scripture Index

Note: Page numbers followed by "n" indicate notes.

About the Authors

Warren W. Wiersbe is a Bible teacher, conference speaker, and author of more than 150 books, including the popular BE series of commentaries on every book of the Bible. Dr. Wiersbe, the former senior pastor of Moody Church in Chicago, served as general director of Back to the Bible for five years. In 2002 he received the Gold Medallion Lifetime Achievement Award from the Evangelical Christian Publishers Association. He and his wife, Betty, have four grown children and reside in Lincoln, Nebraska.

David Wiersbe is pastor of the Clear Lake Evangelical Free Church in Clear Lake, Illinois, where he has served as chaplain to a Fire and Rescue Unit for twelve years. His most extensive counseling and support group experience is with bereaved parents. He and his wife, Susan, have one son, Jonathan.